# *Trevor Beer's* NATURE WATCH

**3**

*With illustrations by the author and Endymion Beer*

ryelands

First published in Great Britain in 2012

British Library Cataloguing-in-Publication Data
A CIP record for this title is available from the British Library

ISBN 978 1 906551 31 5

**RYELANDS**
Halsgrove House,
Ryelands Business Park,
Bagley Road, Wellington, Somerset TA21 9PZ
Tel: 01823 653777   Fax: 01823 216796
email: sales@halsgrove.com

Part of the Halsgrove group of companies
Information on all Halsgrove titles is available at: www.halsgrove.com

Printed and bound by Short Run Press, Exeter

# *Foreword*

**by Alan Qualtrough**
**Editor of the *Western Morning News***

Trevor Beer has written his Nature Watch column in the *Western Morning News* for two decades and it is a must-read for the tens of thousands of *Western Morning News* readers who enjoy the South West countryside.

He is a cherished 'ever present' for us, just like the changeable weather, dramatic landscape and the wild creatures of the Westcountry he writes about.

Trevor's living subjects range from the awesome to the ordinary and all he writes about is bound to delight. He dutifully serves our readers by delivering the sights and the sounds of the countryside literally to their breakfast tables each morning.

Trevor has a special relationship with his readers who write in daily with tales from their own gardens and wildlife worlds; with sightings and observations or for just plain advice. This is because of his deep understanding of the natural history of the Westcountry and his ability to communicate his respect and concern for wild animals and the habitats in which they thrive.

All this has made him one of the best loved and longest serving columnists the *Western Morning News* has ever had.

# Introduction

Nature Watch 3! Who would have thought it? But yer tis, 20 years on thanks to the *Western Morning News* and its readers, and to nature. And to my family and Endymion, my pal and colleague, who put up with my idiosyncrasies in loving nature and our Westcountry flora and fauna above all else. But we need to do so – it is imperative and vital we retain a close link with nature. If we do not, then we fall.

My thanks also to Halsgrove Publishers for producing this set of three tomes, perhaps even a couple more?

When I wrote my very first article for the *Western Morning News* I did not dare to dream that twenty years would go by with me staying in there. But yer tis. So my thanks also to the many readers, some of whom have become friends. I love you and owe you all!

**Cheers! Have a muggatee. Ansome!**
**Trevor Beer MBE**
**North Devon. 2012**

The lone ringed plover looked out of place somehow at the edge of the mudflats for there were literally thousands of other birds of various species as far as the eye could see. The loner in the crowd, and as a non-gregarious soul myself I could feel for her, or him. It is likely there will be a few more about as the winter wears on but hereabouts they are never abundant.

The bird was there at the beginning of our walk, there later on our return, holding to a short area of mud and sand which would soon enough be covered with tide flow.

As a breeding bird the ringed plover has declined in the Westcountry, its pebble and shingle habitat remaining but nowadays heavily pressured by people with more leisure time and the ability to get to beaches easily. The motor vehicle's availability to the masses, the invention of the wheel, shall we say? Well, the wheel was in Nature just waiting to be shaped and used, as most things were or are.

Or are. That's close to 'oo-ar' a bit of Westcountry dialect for 'oh, yes' which has me down off my soap box thank goodness. It's draughty up there.

In the 1970s I could find a dozen breeding pairs of ringed plover in North Devon each year. I doubt anyone could do that now. One of the best places was along the line of sand dunes at Braunton Burrows, and even in some of the 'slacks' amongst the dunes.

The little bird uses a shallow nesting depression. Usually four eggs are laid in May, with incubation about 24 days by both adults. Fledging may be anywhere twixt 23-35 days. Two broods may be raised in one year if the birds can find some seclusion.

Red Deer: once upon a time one of the most important animals in our economy, but that was in prehistoric times, and could be found pretty well everywhere in the countryside. Vastly important in that they provided meat, antlers and bones used for tools, and skins for clothes and other uses. It is known that the Neolithic flint mining people of Grime's Graves in Norfolk used over 50 000 antlers as picks.

It was the advance of farming that brought about deer declines and by the Middle Ages red deer were uncommon in England in terms of abundance. Royal Forests and Parks brought a semi-domesticated status to red deer but fallow deer swiftly took over as the more abundant and more easily managed species.

The decline of the Forest system saw red deer almost dying out in England. Come the late nineteenth century they were more or less confined to the North and on Exmoor, save for a few parks still having herds.

Today, of course, Exmoor's red deer remain famous, drawing many tourists to the area as do those in Scotland where they are controlled by systematic management. The red deer of the Westcountry, though commonest on Exmoor, may be found in many other areas including on Dartmoor. I frequently see red deer outside Exmoor, a magnificent sight and I do hope they will be around forever, as indeed they should be as part of our native fauna.

When out and about try to get used to scanning moor and farmland at a distance, with a binocular. Very often creatures you want to see, but don't, saw you coming as it were. Deer can 'melt' into the landscape despite their large size and are often missed by mere seconds. Don't advertise your presence and do have binoculars.

The stone single-arched bridge twixt field and wood edge cannot be seen by those who wander over it unless they clamber down to the water's edge. In fact few know there is a bridge, so inconspicuous is it, yet it is beautifully made in stones from the old quarry in the wood itself. I have crossed it thousands of times man and boy, watched dippers nest beneath it as they still do, and sat hidden beside it just enjoying the seclusion and the green-ness behind a curtain of Himalayan balsam.

Now on a cold winter's day a pair of coal tits clamber about the stone arch edge, picking insects from hidden recesses where grows harts-tongue and wall rue ferns. Wall rue, once called tentwort and white maidenhair is a lovely fern but being small is often overlooked. I have found it growing in Scotland, in the Cairngorms, and there it grows to its fullest glory, a very pretty fern.

When leading wildlife walks it is a fern I specially look out for. Like black spleenwort and rusty back ferns it is not well known yet so much part of the greenery of the lovely Westcountry. As we wander the countryside in winter we soon become aware of how much green-ness we owe to the delightful presence of ferns.

Someone once said to me how hard it is to learn the different ferns but it is all a matter of application. Don't rush it, learn say, one each weekend taking time to study it in its habitat. Sketch or photograph the fern, look it up in books, befriend it, then move on to another and so on. You will love the ferns and the places where they grow, I feel sure. Happy fern hunting!

Cold wind, clouds converging from two directions, peculiar sight, eerie almost as pink and grey-brown they moved against the blue sky patches. Across the river the park lies green, muddy and empty of people. Only pigeons and jackdaws searched about hopefully as a few herring gulls glide overhead.

The old campshedding retaining the riverbank is green, a mix of moss and slime as the tide ebbs here from its highest reach. Mallard, a muscovy duck and a red-breasted merganser swim or waddle unseen by people in a never-ending flow of traffic. A river of people in metal boxes on wheels, their ebb and flow passing and repassing over the causeway.

A grey heron stands hunched by the river upstream of the road bridge. It doesn't look particularly alert but it may have eaten and is just watching the water. Further up by a former mill another is staring intently down, and yet another by the weir. Each grey bird spaced out along the waterway in its own fishing spot, fish swimming the gauntlet of spearing bills.

No doubt they know each other well, the herons. Probably they are from the same heronry, my guess being Arlington Lake, the address of many herons over scores of years. The heronry there by the lake at this lovely National Trust property is a sight and sound not to miss. Do have it on your places to visit list, both for the heronry and the delightful circular walk. I have led numerous guided walks there with never a discontented walker, all thrilled by the scenery and wildlife. Many came back to take longer holidays or again as part of our walking tours – the Westcountry always a 'pull' to all, locals and visitors alike. Ansome!

From Exmoor to Dartmoor and the lovely Dart valley with Luckey Tor. It is one of my favourite places, having that awesomely beautiful feel for which Dartmoor is so well known. For fine views of the Dartmoor reave system go to Combestone Tor to see those above the river Dart. Magic!

In summer watch wheatears here, and maybe a merlin. Or go to Grimspound on Hamel Down NW of Widecombe-in-the-Moor, special places all. The round pounds could well be for the safe keeping of stock in the days when wolves still roamed. You can just imagine a fire lit here at night, and the tough lives of those who looked after domestic animals.

I once watched a pair of merlins at the clapper bridge over the Wallabrook, a wild place indeed, but they flew off toward distant hills.

Obviously a mated pair they were on the hunt for a nesting site I feel. At this time of year they will be in lower lying, more amenable countryside. Sensible birds.

I usually find them nesting in former nests of other species such as crows. In fact I once found a pair in a former crows nest that had had kestrels use it the previous summer, so quite a motley crew all in one rowan tree over the years. They are said to have taken over eagle's nests in Scotland and even in a duck nest-box formerly occupied by goldeneye!

Ground nesting by merlins was fairly common on the moors, amongst heather. Only one brood of young is raised each year so if mishaps occur all is lost that year. With incubation taking a month or so and fledging taking up to 27 days such birds need peace and seclusion. Our smallest falcon the merlin.

10pm. Cold wintry night. A telephone call. Two swans locked together by their necks, swimming in circles just off the river bank. They are held by discarded fishing lines, wrapped tight about their necks, beaks agape as they fight to free themselves. Off we go to rescue them, two birds undoubtedly frightened and most probably in some pain.

What to do? The night is dark but a fullish moon shines on the river, the street lighting on the Longbridge helping us to see the problem. The tide is on the ebb, the natural river current pushing the two swans in against the left bank and fortunately that is the side we are on. We do not have much equipment. I have a walking stick and an old torch, some rope that has seen better days, and enthusiasm to help wildlife.

It is 11pm. We have been out for an hour or more. The swans are in close to the bank. No telling if they are a 'pair' but it looks as if they are. They revolve and are not at all aggressive with one another. I toss out some bread on to the water and with a flurry in they come. Necks grabbed, wings held down to their sides they submit to being cut free. There is no plastic line down inside their throats. They have been unlucky yet lucky, the line oddly holding both. My guess is one tried to free the other and both became caught.

Back on the water they glance back at us then swim off towards the north bank and the mouth of the Yeo River. We are soaked through, muddy, freezing with cold and delighted. To not have reached them would have been awful for them, miserable for all of us.

Bucketing down with rain but when you have a dog companion 'out' is the operative word. I love rain so Willow, knowing I'm daft enough to walk miles in it, nips on to the return route pretty smartish. Robin song never fails or flags despite the downpour. If anything it adds to the water sounds, a silvery sweetness, a cascade of melody from some ivied shelter.

Readers have asked recently about badgers and squirrels hibernating; they don't. They may well become less active in cold weather yet even in this heavy rain I've seen half a dozen about the bird table. No doubt somewhere in the dense ivy, sheltering the singing robins and other birds, there will be brimstone butterflies hibernating in their adult stage.

The very last one I saw in 2003 flew into the ivy and honeysuckle mass growing over our garden totem pole. I reckon it is there now, wings closed, resembling ivy leaves, just awaiting the spring. If there's a sunny, warm spell in February or March we may see a few on the wing but come a cold snap and back into shelter they'll go for a few more days.

A wren flits into the ivy cover out of the rain, so close yet ignoring us as the unceasing rain beats harder.

*But never mind, this ivy for an hour,*
*Rain as it may, will keep us drily here,*
*That little wren knows well his sheltering bower,*
*Nor leaves his covert, though we come so near.*

The words of John Clare, the great country poet observer of nature.

No let up in the weather so up through the woods we trudge along with a flock of long-tailed tits and a few blue and great tits. They are all calling away merrily, seeking food. Ansome!

Followed a dozen redwings along the lane which here was sheltered by the clay banks of a Devon hedge rich in ferns and other vegetation. The redwings were not having it too easy, the lack of fruit on the trees and shrubs in this area very noticeable back in autumn. Very few haws, acorns or beech nuts, whilst in other areas things were quite good. Yet we had had a good blackberry year with much fruit very early in the season. My view, not enough rain by far when the trees really needed it. It will be interesting to see how things go this year.

The old wooden gate, green with age, is firmly held by an iron hook catch resting in an iron 'staple' embedded in the gate post. A rusty chain and padlock helps secure it, the whole a beautiful picture that no new, red-painted metal gate will ever surpass. No footprints in the gateway mud, no human prints that is, but along the lane are deer slots and the tracks of a badger clearly discernable, all fresh as if the two species had gone for a night stroll together. No doubt they see each regularly on night-time forays for food, a gap between hawthorns showing where they and other wild creatures clamber through.

The redwings had joined a larger flock in the field, a twittering chattering sound emanating from them, then up and away to seek food. Known as a wintering Scandinavian thrush to our shores, the redwing is breeding increasingly in Scotland. I found a pair nesting near Carrbridge one June, on the ground in the shelter of a bush and rowan tree, so could observe them feeding four young.

Almost at the end of the lane, in the field, is the old shed where I have often sheltered from rain. Twas a surprise to find the window panes gleaming, the old pile of books gone, including the Richmal Crompton *Just William* book that had gathered dust on a shelf for years.

But a bird feeder hung from the projecting roof, two blue tits swinging from it, pecking away at peanuts. The nut feeder was well placed to be visible from the window so I just had to peer inside. Table and chair, notepads, a box of pencils, and there were the books now neatly arranged on a tidy shelf on the wall. Some youngsters den-cum-hide for nature watching, the new padlock on the door, signs of recent occupancy and new use of this rather nice old shed.

Willow sniffed about but there was no one 'home'. A trifle cold probably but so good to see a quiet use being made of the building once more. Some wonderful sightings would be had from here I had no doubt.

Inside at one window corner a harvestman moved one of its eight legs. Sheds, compost heaps, upturned flower pots, all attract this relative of spiders which feeds on living and recently-dead insects. They will also take fungi or other vegetation.

To escape predation themselves harvestmen will occasionally sacrifice a leg. This continues to wriggle which may hold the attention of the would be predator, allowing the harvestman to escape capture.

They are found in woods, grassland and short vegetation, conspicuous in autumn hence their English name, and often about after rain. Eggs hatch as miniature adults in form but take about nine months to mature.

"Where can I find willow tits?" asked a local birdwatcher. Well there's a question. Actually they are found in the same habitats as marsh tits broadly speaking but they do like damp woodlands with secondary shrub growth and plenty of old, rotting timber for them to hack out their nest sites. The willow tit is scarce, much rarer than the marsh tit, and best sought in the breeding season where it likes to nest in elder and alder tree holes. I have also found them in moist conifer plantations in North Devon.

Getting to know bird songs and calls helps a great deal with bird identification. The best way to do that is by being out listening and watching from early spring. There are some good recordings available on CDs and tapes but nothing beats being amongst it and learning for yourself by careful observation.

Perhaps the best example is differentiating twixt chiff chaff and willow warbler in the field. These warblers are very similar in appearance and as summer visitors move amongst tree foliage from April to September. However their songs are remarkably different, rendering it impossible to misidentify the birds. And is it not remarkable in itself that the many various birds do have different songs and plumages? Whilst we can blandly say 'why' in our own way of thinking, it is nevertheless exciting, a fascinating aspect of nature.

Go out and listen to the Robin's song change from winter silver to summer gold. Hark to the blackbird and thrush as spring has them break into song, or to the more urgent sounding calls of the tit family. Let it all in. To fill your own days with bird song, the humming of bees, to seek out the scents of flowers. Ansome!

More by accident than design is a common enough phrase and for the nature lover it is often appropriate. This morning I was checking an ash tree I had planted in a hurry during rain, in memory of a friend's cat that had just died. I had made a good enough job of the planting but it is always worthwhile to check to see all is well. I took out my spade and decided a bit more tamping down of the soil would be a good idea I pushed the spade into a mound of earth to do some heeling in. As I did so some soil fell away from a narrow tunnel and five richly brown beetles were exposed.

The insects moved in single file deeper into the tunnel, which I believe was a mouse run, and were soon gone but not before I'd had a good look. Luckily I had my camera with me to take a picture of the tree so managed a shot of the beetles together. Then home to the books, a short search revealing the beetles were *Trechus quadristriatus*, a common species in Britain. The species lives in fields and meadows, often living underground, and common or not I was well pleased with the find on a winter's day.

These unusual incidents, serendipitous as they are, make one's day. I went off to find a cardboard tube, put it in place against the tunnel I'd inadvertently damaged and firmed a mound of soil over and all around it. Then I carefully pulled the tube away, thankful the soil was wet and moulded nicely about it. It came away perfectly. The tunnel and mound repaired, the tree well planted, I felt I deserved a cuppa, and learnt a lot. Ansome!

I enjoy watching rabbits. Evening time is usually good for that. Farm gate just right for elbows and for Willow to gaze through. Hereabouts rabbits have moved house as rabbits field has been largely under water for quite a while. Presently they are living on higher, drier land with ideal earth banks and dense bramble for cover.

An important source of food during the early twentieth century and through the two wars, rabbit provided thousands of people with stews and pies when they would have gone somewhat hungrier methinks.

Though litters of up to seven young can be produced every four or five weeks it doesn't happen that way usually. Indeed in a situation where the population density is too high the birth rate is controlled by the unborn young being re-absorbed by the mother's body.

So why did we have 'too many' a few decades ago? To the extent that humans deliberately spread the awful disease myxomatosis to decimate the rabbit population?

Well firstly it was 'too many' from our point of view, not the rabbits', who found their numbers sustainable in the countryside with plenty of food and shelter. Also we were still killing them for food at an amazing rate, whereby the rabbits continued to multiply and replenish their numbers.

Now endemic in many districts myxomatosis breaks out on occasions and is part and parcel of the modern rabbit's life, the disease being what we might today term 'a weapon of mass destruction' in that it was deliberately introduced with that purpose.

But if you are considering studying a particular animal as part of nature watching the rabbit lends itself ideally to regular, all year round observations of great interest. Large enough to be easily observable at a non-disturbance distance you may be pleasantly surprised.

From my vantage point the town was a Sargasso Sea with 'eels' of constant traffic heading for it. Market Day, the main Friday one, with sales in most shops part of the draw.

Two buzzards flew out from the leafless trees to soar in weak sunlight over a wood where buzzards have nested for at least all my years and no doubt centuries more. It is a typical woodland bird, long persecuted by man but fairly adaptable so found at times on open moorland. I know of a few holding territories in mature conifer plantations, but for me buzzard country is farmland with patchwork fields and broadleaved wooded valleys, the best of the varied Westcountry habitats for wildlife richness.

To see buzzards soaring in circles over woods and farmland is to see birds not only holding territory but joyful in living, just as you and I might be on a sunny spring or summer day. In April, eggs will be laid in large stick nests often with a fringe of leafy greenery added, though if it is a cold, wet spring they may lay in May or even later. Incubation is by the female for 33-35 days.

The male keeps watch from a nearby tree, as well as hunting and bringing food to the nest for his mate. Both adults hunt for the young, though it is the female who divides up the food and feeds them. Nestlings become fully fledged at 42-49 days, a family flying together as fine a sight as any in the countryside. The adults may continue to feed or help find food for the young well into autumn. Only one brood is raised each year.

A superb bird of prey, so much part of the Westcountry native fauna.

The banshee-like scream of a water rail from close by had us leaping about. Well it was a water rail-like scream actually as I've never heard a banshee. The marsh water reflected almost black and we could see Orion quivering on the surface as well as in the sky. Earlier about 100 frogs had dipped and bobbed as we passed their spawning ground, and there are daisies in bloom. The countryside is beginning to sing and zing again, the soil restless, about to send all kinds of plants springing skywards.

No telling what had upset the water rail. It is a diurnal species really but as night falls upon the marshes who knows what wild creatures are about seeking shelter or a meal. Earlier, on reaching the frog pool, we had seen a kingfisher fly over the smooth water. Where was it now? It is a bird which does not survive in bitter cold yet almost every single item of food has to be caught beneath the water surface. Small fish, aquatic insects and tiny crustaceans are the kingfisher's food but I saw one take berries long ago.

Come March some will be knocking soil from river banks excavating nest holes. Kingfishers may have three broods in a year but two is more likely. Actually they have done well of late and I see them most weeks, often three or four times in a week.

The water rail is much rarer as a breeding bird but there are a few pairs breeding in the Westcountry. An elegantly attractive bird it is not much bigger than a thrush. The squeals and grunts sometimes emanating from dense marshy vegetation could give one the impression there's a wild boar in the vicinity. Not that that is so unlikely these days.

Three pheasants, a cock and two hens had wandered along the lane and into the woods at sundown. It was cold and I wished in a way I was home but I wanted to watch the pheasants. In ten minutes they were up in two trees silhouetted against the distant silver river. They could have been an old rookery to anyone who hadn't seen them fly up, sway seemingly precariously, one with a bit of wing beating to balance, then settle down. The lower tree branches are stout, taking their weight easily. Crows and wood pigeons roost higher, the latter loving the conifers.

The pheasants feel safe. I reckon the shadows and gloom below them are as a blanket would be to us, a comfort. No fox will catch them tonight. Come daylight they will fly down into cover and will be heard calling occasionally, yet for such large birds they are not seen as often as the small tits and finches, or even the dunnocks who spend more time on the ground, as do the pheasants.

A crescent moon and Venus shining so bright I have to stand and stare, an incredible sight our brightest planet, a moment of magic, made more so by the geese chatting gently on the river. Night falls fast in winter as if the sun wants to get its head down out of the cold.

There is a badger drinking at the Dripping Well. It pauses, remaining still, watching Willow and I walk quietly by, up over the wood path. Willow is not a botherer of wild creatures, he has more sense. The people who walk their dogs here by day rarely see the badger or fox. Some have never seen either in the wild. I am glad I can tell you about them.

Could not believe the ferocity of the weather! And I've been around a while. May be it is seemingly different as I approach 27 years yet again. Do you know the old saying from Roman times? Hells bells and buckets of blast?!

Well that's how it was as we left Cornwall to head back over into Devon with the car literally rocking in the wind and rain. Dearie me! Pendeen and that area seems to be in a micro-climate for it was sunny and sweet. Yet all around and on the way home it was black, seriously weatherbeaten and wild. But Pendeen and that area an interesting pocket of warmth and sunshine in an otherwise rather bleakly beautiful landscape.

Used to seeing red deer on Exmoor, it was just a bit odd to see a dozen hinds way down in Cornwall even though one knows they get about a bit, as do roe deer. I feel the recent muntjac 'scare' is a bit far fetched however, a report saying they are responsible for nightingale declines. This is elsewhere than the Westcountry of course, the nightingale a very scarce species in the South West and virtually non-existent in my home area. I used to go over to Minehead and West Quantoxhead area to see nightingales and nightjars, they are that few and far between.

Muntjac are tiny deer, around 18ins (45cms) at the shoulder and not easy to observe as they prefer to stay in the undergrowth. It is an introduced species, originally from China. Young are born at any time of the year. A naturalist who writes from France tells me they are doing well there but are not causing any hardship to other wildlife species. The muntjac is a browser on bramble and such.

It had drizzled all day with a fair bit of wind so everywhere was wet and soggy. We had walked across a favourite valley to a footpath by a stream and orchard. A well-built shed afforded some shelter when the rain came on heavy so we tucked ourselves in against it to wait out the worst of the weather.

Just as well we did or we'd have missed over 40 ladybirds tucked up snugly inside against the window frame. They were all 2-spot ladybirds, a not uncommon species and one I have found overwintering on tree trunks in bark crevices, and in fence posts from time to time, often in hundreds. The 2-spot ladybird seems to be attracted to cool locations in buildings but it is difficult to assess why they tend to group unless it is simply a case of winter habitat availability. It is thought by some that the scent of pheromones attract them and numbers swiftly build up.

I once found many hundreds of 7-spot ladybirds in a huge grass tussock surrounding the gatepost at the sanctuary, our private nature reserve, and a similar large group in dense gorse on a south-facing slope. There has to be a common attraction for so many tiny beetles to locate each other and group together all winter. Usually some leave the group beginning in February or March, and all are gone by, or during, April.

Adult ladybirds live for about a year and though we associate them with summer they may be found in all months of the year. They do become inactive during the autumn and winter, building up their fat reserves, often by eating alternative foods as their preferred diet becomes scarce, so could be around seven months old when about in the spring.

Moving away from the sheltering shed with its cluster of ladybirds there was a slight movement in the orchard corner furthest from us. Chickens? I wondered, but no, my binocular showed a covey of partridges. Typically they keep to the ground in this damp, misty weather, remaining silently in a huddle.

Coveys hold together and if anything does part the birds all it takes is a rasping little call like stones being scraped together and the birds will group again. I love to watch partridges on fine summer days, always have, even if a bird is nesting along a hedge and not doing much. Well, it is what summer days and high grass movements are for, not doing much yet taking in all the scents, sounds and sights. Til then we have the spring before us, a Westcountry spring, perfect.

Years ago I remember a couple of local poachers who would fly a kite over fields with partridges in them, at weekends with their two kids. The birds would lay low, just as they'd do with a raptor hovering above and in across the field would go the fellow not controlling the kite or its string. Partridges for tea for someone. Not that they filled a plate but the local gentry paid for them at back doors and I guess they went down well with dinner and a bottle of port.

No. I did not get involved. My love for partridges it that they are alive. Tiny little birds with immense charm. I report it as it is. Same as with moorhens eggs and such. There was a 'posh' market and country folk availed themselves of it, some as buyers, some as sellers. It is the same today in fact. Pussyfooting around the facts gets nobody nowhere. Pardon the grammar.

Moving on from the siskins in the alder trees, I walked up the lane with Willow where I used to meet up with Bill. It is a strange feeling knowing he wont be there anymore, least ways not as he was, but in spirit perhaps he may be at times, revisiting old haunts. I shall look and listen for him.

Sometimes I'd scan the waterway with my binocular and find him sitting with a fishing rod by the stream. He was good at trout fishing yet I often felt he was as happy just watching the river, whether he caught supper or not. Sometimes I'd creep down to where he sat, back in my days with dear old Bracken, and he'd say, "Buzz off for a minute, they'm nibbling at the bait".

I would sit down with Bracken and watch. Sure enough, if a fish was nibbling, Bill would be on to it and afore long the aroma of a fish supper would be all a part of the little cottage in its North Devon valley. A few times we'd sit outside on a summer's eve eating with our fingers at trout cooked on a brick oven in the garden, with fresh bread and butter and a glass of home-made gorse flower wine. It doesn't come any better than that. The rule, 'take a drink when eating fish', is one to obey. Common sense and fresh bread and butter, well, who would do without?!

We got on so well. He'd grin at me and tell me I'd never catch a fish with binoculars. Tis true. But I'm no hunter-gatherer and rely on our farmers who feed us all so well. We bought potatoes and free range eggs at a local farm this week, with a sign on the roadside. Good spuds too, perfect for roasting.

Jasper our Tabby travelled from this plane of living on February 16th, a stray who wandered into the porch one stormy night, and decided the old guy who dried him and cuddled him may be the answer to his searching for a new home. So he stayed, and now years later on to his journeying he goes. Readers write to tell of their cats and dogs, some of parrots, some of the pet rabbits and sheep, and especially of the wildlife in their gardens. A fine, delightful cat, Jasper, bless him.

Endymion has been cleaning off the garden wall along the front of our home as it needed painting to catch up with the rest of the house, freshly done last autumn. Going out to see how it was coming along it was looking good, the scraping down, but not very fast. "Can't rush it," she said, "lots of chiggy-pigs, centipedes and things so I'm rescuing them all and seeing they have a new home before I carry on." Ansome!

Chiggy pigs are woodlice of course, nice little creatures who like moist areas so are often found beneath log piles and such. Lots of garden snails, hiding in the ivy, interesting creatures all if we but give them time of day.

And what names science gives to creatures and plants. The yellow centipede with its dark head and first few segments is *Necrophaeophagus longicornis*, and is found in the soil of gardens and fields throughout Britain. What a name to be lumbered with.

Centipedes emerge at night, hiding in dark places by day, beneath bark, in leaf litter, and as we found, in wall crevices. If a centipede is exposed to dry, sunny conditions it will die in a few hours, hence Endymion's urgency to rescue them.

Well the old belief that birds are paired up by February 14th, St Valentine's Day, was certainly true in this neck of the woods. Now as February draws to a close, at least as I write this that is, so we have early birds with nest material going to and fro, including our resident house sparrows.

It is spring. Whatever calendars say the signs are all about that the land is awakening, even if we do get some wind chill on occasions. Saw a brimstone butterfly and a small tortoiseshell on February 18th, on the wing before the nor'easters turned up. Such early flyers, out of hibernation, quickly find shelter again if needs be.

Saw a cream-coloured badger too. The animal was in a wild area in a spinney just across from a wood. Thankfully left wild by its land owner the site is quite rich in wildlife with a few rarities on board. Let us hope and pray it stays farmed and does not become 'opened up' for the public beyond just the odd public right of way being maintained. As nice as it seems to 'open up' the countryside more and more for the general public some of the so-called nature conservation activities being promoted by large sums of Euro-cash, for example, are counter productive when it comes to wildlife conservation and species recovery from the very real and serious declines. Less people pressure would help at this time, not more. Give it twenty years of more wilderness and let us then see if we can afford to create people habitat by eradicating wildlife habitat in the countryside.

The cream badger ambled off ghost-like into the undergrowth. Not an omen I hope, ghosts of badgers but no real ones remaining!

Snow and ice, pretty on postcards but things to beware of in reality. Frankly I don't mind them too much as long as cold winds do not moan over the land at the same time. In fact you can keep your cold winds at any time, is my view, though no doubt our Maker has good reason for them, some say. Down to the river to find a few birds dead as usual under these conditions. If you find a few then there are many more nearby and other creatures too.

It was getting dimpsey as we wandered homeward to the weird musical strains of a full orchestra of geese, hidden from view by a shower of sleet and hail skimming upriver and pattering amongst the soaking black trees of the woods. Someone has obviously been papering the rooms of their house. To do that in January surely brings snow.

"When frost and snow are both together, sit by the fire and spare shoe leather," is an old saying which makes a lot of sense; but a snow year is a rich year for the farmer, tis said. Odd how old sayings come to mind at such moments and indeed as we wandered along the creek at Fremington we met a local fisherman.

"Can hardly talk," he croaked. "Have got an awful sore throat".

"Shame on you," I told him. "Go home and pour boiling water over blackcurrant jam. Easy stuff to obtain. Then take drinks of the resulting blackcurrant tea when your throat hurts. It'll soon go." Why local country folk don't know these remedies I just don't know. Everyone, town or country dweller should have a book of country cures. I shall just have to get round the editor to let me write a real series of country wisdom.

The merlin, a little male, was perched on a fence post looking quite splendid in winter sunshine with the white snow-sprinkled field behind him. Hard to think of them catching pigeons yet their scientific name, *Falco columbarius* tells of this, Columba being a pigeon, a dove.

Occasionally I get into the mood to learn a few scientific names for wild species though I find it easy to lapse. I used to look the names up of the birds, plants and animals I saw of a day and attempt to learn them, but I have one of those brains that let slip such matters.

Today I went in search of a bittern which has been observed not far from home but failed to find it. But the merlin was a bonus. Bittern, our European species is *Botanus stellaris*. Boo is Latin for I cry aloud, or roar, and Taurus being bull, tells us that the bird's weird call is likened to that of a roaring bull. Stellaris is starry, referring to the spots in the bird's plumage though it will be seen to be more streaky than starry.

The bittern is about in this neck of the woods due to harder weather conditions elsewhere in the British Isles and probably came on the cold easterly winds that hit us recently. NE winds mostly, but the way they moaned along our lane was decidedly from the east, whatever the forecasts showed.

However, cold as it was and is, many birds are in summer plumage and they wont change now. Our chaffinches, for example, are quite colourful, the males resplendent in full breeding plumage, and many a black-headed gull is smartly attired with that dark chocolate head which is so distinctive in the species, prior to breeding.

Bush vetch in full flower on February 26th, by the way, along with a skriddick of Shepherd's Purse blooming near the old Dripping Well. Here, too, was golden saxifrage and plenty of fresh stinging nettles, a lovely sight at a rather cold time.

A drunken fellow swayed through the metal kissing gates by the Well, to lurch across, hold his head down to a hastily picked plant leaf and drink from the water pouring along it. That is the trick at the Well as the water issues out from a rock crevice and vertically downward. So, you pick a plantain or other sturdy leaf, place it in the crevice to bring the water further out, and fill your bottle. This fellow had not brought the bottles with him that had contributed to his inebriated condition and had now dropped to one knee in the icy water to continue his quaffing. Willow stared.

Noticing me watching the fellow grinned vacantly and said, "Good for your eyes you know. You should try it. Wearing those glasses you need it. Did they call you four-eyes at school?"

"Not unless they wanted a clip round the ear," I replied.

He dunked his other knee in the shallow pool and looked down in surprise. "Good for your eyes you know. I don't wear glasses."

"You are supposed to bathe your eyes with the water, not drink it," I told him, hopefully helpfully.

"Oooh! Are you? Too cold for that." He rose and lurched on up the hill, his trousers and shoes soaked, singing a song, quite tunefully actually. Willow watched him go with what I feel sure was a look of bewilderment on his handsome face. But then, he had cocked his leg in the pool earlier. It is a funny old world.

Rascal the tabby is, like all cats, pretty intelligent. He has half moved in with us now. Well, all of him comes in but he chooses when, eats well, then wanders about in the back garden. Occasionally Willow walk-chases him around the paths to show him who's boss. Other cats in the avenue know Willow wouldn't harm them so they all adopt this strange head-down trot which looks fast but isn't, whilst Willow just herds them out in true sheepdog manner, but casually.

Rascal and dear old Jasper got on well and now Rascal spends longer and longer with us, knowing the sounds of crockery and cutlery and the scents of real cooking. Today I put him a shelf on our fence and a pole sloping up to it as I noticed he sat up there in the sunshine. Sure enough, up he went, scent-marked the shelf with his chin and washed his paws and ears. Then he dozed off. A while later when I looked he'd moved, following the sunny spots as they changed with the sun's movement across the sky. A solar energy expert as are butterflies, lizards and such.

It rather looks as if Rascal has left his former home and is moving in. He pinches my armchair with cushions, in the den and I move on to the harder chair. He reckons it's good for my back trouble. I do declare he may be right as posture is important.

Cats like to be high up. They love good vantage points in order to see over their domain. Willow likes a cat pal as long as we give the nod the cat is OK. Otherwise they are moved on which helps the garden wildlife species who rely on him as a sort of bouncer.

A single fieldfare perched in the lone hawthorn, a fairy tree, by the flooded gulley of rabbit field. No crimson haws lit the bare branches and on our return the bird was gone. Its place was taken by a pair of chaffinches, the male splendid in breeding plumage, the female quite green looking. She will be well camouflaged when their neat nest is built, perhaps in the hawthorn itself. Below the finches a pair of mallard float, drifting on the water of the gulley which is fringed by rushes, the male's head glinting that rich bottle green we always see in sunshine.

On a gean, or wild cherry tree, is a hairy, rather robust moth which is barred and speckled with browns and yellows of varying hues. It is perched at only 6ft so we can look closely at its beauty of colour and form. In fact its English name is Brindled Beauty, a moth usually early on the wing in March and April when it likes to rest on tree trunks. The male of the species is attracted to light so it is more often than not seen by us at our homes than out in the wild. I have seen Brindled Beauty caterpillars on fruit trees, especially pear trees and it is not an uncommon moth.

Like the closely related but scarcer Oak Beauty, the Brindled is very variable and easily missed on its tree bark perch. It is one of the geometers, the caterpillars 'looping' as they walk. Remember the words of an old song, "inchworm, inchworm, measuring the marigold." Songs were pretty once.

The gean is a common tree in this particular woodland, the shiny bark glowing, proclaiming its presence amongst the oaks. It is a treat to see its early spring blossom and later the small but attractive cherry fruits.

Apples give pleasure in so many ways. Raw or in a good old country-style pie, in a fruit salad, and as food for birds, butterflies and other wildlife. Frances Quantz of Crownhill, Plymouth, writes of putting apples out on the grass, with one in the 'feeding bush'. A pair of blackcaps have been feeding on the apple in the bush whilst blackbirds and a song thrush demolish the ground supply. With the ground apple finished one blackbird did a balancing act from the one in the bush.

I have been watching the acrobatics of a blackbird in our garden. With the more reachable ivy berries gone he has been flying from the fence and in passing the ivied area he does a sideways flip and grabs a berry. This has become a regular feeding method so no doubt others will soon copy him. 'Learning' is fascinating to watch. Rascal the tabby has been closely watching the grey squirrels going up and down the ladder I put in place twixt fence and bird table. I thought his idea was to hunt and chase a squirrel at some stage, but no. Along the fence top he went this morning, down the ladder rung by rung, sniffed around at the goodies, then deciding they were not to his taste, he walked back up the ladder, thence to top shed roof to continue watching over his new domain.

Saw a crow in an oak struggling to snip a twig for its nest as its mate watched nearby. The bird succeeded after a while, obviously determined to have that particular stick. Crows usually nest just 100 yards or so from our home so there's always lots of interesting goings on to see. Never a dull moment, nature watching, I reckon.

Along the beach the tiny piles of sand betray the whereabouts of lug-worms but today there were no fishermen or women digging bait. It is moist stuff so adheres to form a string like coil. Close by is a small pit about 2.5cms (1ins) across with a minute hole in its floor. The coil and pit mark the two ends of the U shaped burrow and it is here the lug worm lives. After swallowing sand the worm extrudes the inedible remains on to the surface thereby telling us of its presence.

The lug-worm is quite a sedentary character and once safely buried it rarely moves. Even when reproducing it sends its spawn up through the burrow into the sea. Rhythmical expansion and contraction of its segments pumps water through its tunnel. Lug-worms are also known as lob-worms.

Actually there are several types of seashore worm including some related to our land earthworm. Some like the lug-worm are sedentary, rarely moving far all their lives whilst others are errant, meaning they can swim or crawl more or less freely. These latter types have a head which may bear a number of organs, mostly used for feeling, and some may have rudimentary eyes. They can thrust their throat outside their mouth, using it to collect food, some having jaws which could give us a nip if we are not careful.

Waders exploit these worms and other creatures in the soil as food, the largest, the curlew, using its long, sensitive bill to good effect in its probing quest for bivalves and worms. It is useful to remember that the bills of these birds are much more than mere hard, dagger-like food probers, they actually feel the prey they are seeking, as well as catch it.

On the beach just below the foredunes the clear trail of a fox could be followed to where it turned inland to lope off amongst the dunes. Light rain swept onshore, marram grass waving in the breeze, and tonight brown rats will scavenge the tideline eating anything that comes their way, including our washed-up food refuse and the eggs and young of seabirds.

Out in the water two common seals watched us large-eyed and beautiful, floating shorewards, heads shining and short muzzled as the sea lapped gently along the shoreline. They frequent sand banks and estuaries whilst the more pointed nosed grey seals seem to prefer rocky coasts. Both species may be seen around our Westcountry shores but are often overlooked. We saw a grey seal in Cornwall which must have been all of 8ft in length.

Looking along the wide empty expanse of sand as we walk it is not easy to imagine the abundance of life beneath the surface of this inter-tidal zone which looks a bit lifeless. Below our feet a variety of animals are seeking food, feeding or just waiting for the next tide. The falling rain, coming on harder though it was, will not alter to any extent the brine in the waterlogged sands below us. Seaweed decaying away, plankton and organic materials; we are walking on a richness of life. Let us hope it remains that way.

Looking back the way we came the two seals are upon the beach still looking our way. I wonder what they make of us? It would be good to go back to put an arm around them, to commune in some way but having learned about mankind generally, they would lollop back into the water and swim away. Sad that.

Inland now from the dunes and seashore, following a retaining bank which reclaimed land in the nineteenth century, for agriculture. Some old rusty huts add to the landscape. It would be awful to see posh new ones. I know a fellow who fished here, who hung his knapsack on a hut door, filled with tasty sandwiches and a flask. When he came back to enjoy them a fox had scoffed the lot, well the eatables, but he had the beverage left him. He needed to lose weight anyway and the fox would have been happy and slept well that night.

I used to row here from a boathouse by Rock Park in Barnstaple. On the tide, going back, especially. It always seemed uphill, the river did, on the way home. Perhaps it is. Like that lovely spot on Exmoor where you can stand and watch a stream flow uphill, an interesting illusion.

In the summer there will be evening primroses and viper's bugloss here in plenty. It has always been so. When I was a lad you could find lapwings in the dune hollows and the skylark song was deafening, lovely.

Isn't it amazing how evening primrose has helped so many people despite the negative attitudes from some scientists? Ansome! I'll may be get a few attack letters as I do with badgers and common ragwort but eventually the truth will out as it always does, and all will be well.

Viper's bugloss, a lovely wildflower, with names such as Blueweed, Blue Thistle, Our Saviour's Flannel and Wild Borage. It is a plant thought to cure snakebite and I have actually seen it used to do so, and help an old friend bitten by an adder! Absolutely true. When you see it work, it works.

What a walk! Just minutes from home and a peregrine falcon flew over, low and easy into a westward wind, in full sunlight so low I could make out the moustachial streak with ease. A couple have been hunting the estuary all winter but so many of the waders have left already that I doubt we will see the falcons here now. They'll be off to the coast for the breeding season. Or some inland quarry. Or a church tower or two.

Then within minutes a kingfisher, perched on a branch left by the tide to span a gully it often fishes. It did not stay long, just stared down into the water, saw its timing was wrong for fish and with a shrill 'peep' was off across the Taw to the mouth of the Yeo River. It can often be seen over there perched on the sterns of boats and doing a bit of fishing.

So I thought for the rest of this week I'll take you on a walk from the river back to my place. Coltsfoot has suddenly bloomed in abundance and we are finding it has spread remarkably swiftly, even up in the woods by the Dripping Well. I wonder how many people think it is a dandelion and walk on by with nary a second glance?

But less obvious still, in bloom, is the tiny Shepherd's Purse, its white flowers barely visible so small is the whole plant. The plants here are in the heart of the wood so hardly the 'persistent weed' it is known as when it pops up in our lawns.

The seeds look like leather purses, hence the English name. It is visited by insects but is self pollinated and is said to have distinctive variations in particular localities, something I must check out.

Saw a bit of a barney going on at the edge of a rough grass field with squeaking much louder than the size of the two adversaries suggested. It was a traditional battle twixt two field voles, their short tails helping identification as did the yellow-brown colouring. The 'battle' such as it was, was more of a squeaking flurry of belligerence than physical and I could see no damage to either combatant. Had they not been so involved when I arrived I doubt if I would have seen them at all, though their runs through the grass are numerous if you know what to look for.

The fact, too, that barn owls hunt over this field at evening time tells of the presence of prey species. No prey, no predators about for long, is the rule.

The field vole's main food is grass, the succulent lower stems being favoured. The little creature will also take bulbs, roots and tree bark at ground level. Field voles are about 4ins (10cms) head and body length, with

a 1½ins (40mm) tail. Damp, tussocky grassland is the favoured habitat, a vole nesting in a conspicuous tussock and having runs among the grass stems in individual but small territories.

Stand still and quiet in such a field, maybe by a hedge and you may hear the loud squeaks and chatterings of field voles going about their business. They are not nocturnal but have 'shifts' of a few hours on and off duty, so to speak.

With normal life span of only a year or so they have to get on with living and young females are ready to mate at six weeks of age. I find nests beneath logs at the Sanctuary at times as I always leave fallen trees lying.

It was raining steadily at 10am but that did not deter the pair of blackbirds building a nest in the garden. As I glanced out of the kitchen window, waiting for the kettle to boil, there was the male with an ivy leaf and a length of dead grass, on the path and looking for more material. This pair are building in the leylandii arch, a popular, well-sheltered early spring location. The nest is in the curve of the arch, at the 'shoulder' as it were. In the front garden another pair have chosen the ledge of a stone wall behind a dense curtain of ivy and a fuchsia bush.

Both spots have had successful nests over at least two decades, as has our laurel hedge to the west side of the property. Busy times, and as soon as I locate an active nest site I keep away as much as possible so as not to disturb the birds and cause them to desert. With such an early start to their nesting it is highly likely the blackbirds will raise three broods in the year, their 'season' often being well into September.

At present robins, dunnocks, blackbirds, collared doves, wood pigeons and song thrushes are nesting in the garden, with these species, plus chaffinch and greenfinch, blue and great tits all nesting just over the fence in the wood behind us. This is my favourite time of year, through to October when all about is buzzing with activity. Tis ansome you.

As soon as I heard the first chiff chaff of the year singing away I felt my own spirits lift. Amazing what a bit of bird song does to chase away any blues one might have. Out and about, rain or shine, the Westcountry, lovely.

Bucketing down with rain, mid afternoon and a bedraggled cock pheasant flew into our garden, sheltered beneath the 'umbrella' fir trees and began preening. It was still there two hours later and looking much better. They are no fools these birds. Along the road another garden had a visit from a red legged partridge, the so-called game birds finding the wilds a bit rough it seems. Even a chiff chaff stayed put in one of our conifers, just watching the downpour; unusual for such a restless little warbler.

Suddenly the few fish in our top pond all died. I found them on top of the water so to speak, just lying there with no visible injuries, all on the same day. I had not been doing any kind of work or activity that could have caused an accidental run off into the water, of anything toxic. Indeed I am a most careful person in that respect so will now have to clean out the pond and redo it all. The frogspawn was looking good too but needs must, the job has to be tackled. If I find the cause I will mention it in a forthcoming 'Nature Watch', as it may help others with the same problems.

In the woods the first wood anemones, or wind flowers, bloomed on March 19th, reluctant to open fully in the pouring rain but telling of the spring and its blessings, including the clocks changing and longer daylight hours. Wind flower an apt name for this fragile looking yet hardy plant of March time, with its very attractive leaves.

Other names for this lovely white-flowered plant include Nemony, Bread, Cheese and Cider, Chimney Smocks, Evening Twilight, Granny Thread The Needle, Silver Bells and Smell Foxes. It does have a peculiar perfume.

The lane above the woods is full of the scent of life now as spring makes herself felt in so many ways. Below us, unseen, a curlew is calling, a few remaining about though most of the waders have gone to breeding haunts. The days have been a bit grim weatherwise but the evenings are more pleasant. As the days lengthen the choice to put in an extra walk or watch

TV is an easy one to make , with Willow as frisky as they make 'em, always ready to go.

The golden gorse flowers are so bright one might think it is they which light the evenings with yellow flame and touch gold into the goldfinches wings.

A pair is nesting in a small clump of trees adjoining the main woodland. It is a young plantation of oaks and alder planted by a school group over a decade ago whereas the main wild wood is centuries old. We have watched the finches quietly going back and forth with the grass, rootlets, fibres, moss and lichen, a lovely sight, the neat nest well made and hidden. In May or perhaps early June 4-6 eggs will be laid and incubated by the female for a fortnight. The young will leave the nest two weeks later after being fed by both adults. Quite often two broods are raised as is the case with most finch species.

I see a pair of moorhens have eggs already, not far from where mallard are building in the marsh, beneath brambles at the edge of a dyke. The highest nesting situation I have seen for mallard was in the former nest of sparrowhawks by a farm gate at Mortehoe, Devon. The nest was about 7ft off the ground not far from lovely Rockham Bay.

Shafts of sunlight stream through the wooden five barred gate, green with moss, as early evening mist lends a mysteriousness to the valley. There is a mist hollow all across the field in a diagonal straight line about 6ft wide. Once this was a packhorse route and now with its pale wraiths veiling the grass it is as if the ghosts of many pack horses and their owners have come out from some spirit world to talk of old times.

I remember snipe in this field but it was a long time ago, back when the farmer would dam the stream briefly to let it flow onto the field and spread to green up the grass. A water meadow, and what buttercups grow there, even nowadays, a wondrous sight.

Beyond the woods is a goyal, a narrow coombe in the hillside. It's like a small world of its own, an oasis but in a green and verdant countryside. Perhaps a bit of green wilderness is a better description. I often 'disappear' here to watch such a wealth of wildlife in one small place it is as if there is a store of life ready in case it is needed elsewhere.

There must be numerous goyals such as this. Thank the gods for them and the fact they are not farmable. It is here, or just nearby that I've watched yellow wagtails nesting in recent years, and enjoyed sharing moments with pearl boarded fritillary butterflies. It is an absolute treasure trove of primroses and violets, wildflowers loved by these insects, and I'm sure by all who see them.

Found some sweet violets in flower, the lovely scent a joy. Our only violet to have a fragrance it is not common but here there was a mass of them, some pure white but mostly the typical rich violet colour we see in rainbows.

Magic moments are far from rare when one is nature watching and this past week has been more than interesting. Over the woods I watched a dozen or more jackdaws flying in fairly casual manner in a group when up behind them comes a sparrowhawk, flying fast and purposefully. The hawk flew by the two daws bringing up the rear and was suddenly amongst the flock. An error of judgement I fear, perhaps a first-year hawk not too well acquainted with the crow family. Uproar ensued, you could have heard the jackdaws a mile away, as they called hoarsely, clamouring as they swerved and zoomed about.

The hawk checked visibly, splaying its wings, using them as brakes and then with even more clamour the jackdaws were on to it as one. The hawk turned tail completely and went off back the way it had come with all the jackdaws flying after it. I lost sight of them then but could hear the racket receding in the distance for a while. I have a feeling the sparrowhawk will think twice before having a go at a flock of jackdaws again. Maybe it had been lucky with a flock of starlings and had mis-identified its quarry. The various crow species are a canny lot and tough with it.

Recently, on the coast, we were caught out by a thunderstorm but luckily the tide was on the ebb so we took shelter in a cave which is quite large within. It was dark but forked lightning lit the interior in subliminal fashion, a weird effect, and there were at least nine jackdaws roosting. It was an irresistible scene so I went home and painted the impression of it left on my mind, including the birds.

Another magic moment following on from the jackdaw and sparrowhawk episode occurred as I watched a wood pigeon eating ivy berries in the same woods. The berries close to the tree trunk up which clambered the ivy had been eaten by various birds so it was all about reaching out for the remainder.

To my utter surprise the wood pigeon swung by its feet to hang completely upside-down whereupon it calmly proceeded to gobble all the berries it could reach in this position. The bird even had one wing extended, presumably to help its balance in this extraordinary position which it maintained for well over a minute.

Whether the pigeon had moved out too far on to ivy too thin to hold its weight, then in slipping held on to find itself head down, with the berries available and its grip firm I shall not know lest I see it occur again. But accident or design, the bird held on for a meal and quite easily righted itself afterwards. A sight to remember.

Ivy berries come along at a most useful time to help many a wild creature survive from winter into early spring. A good plant in many ways it is still used by a few as a Christmas and a May Day decoration, along with holly at the former of course. A friend in Ireland still uses ivy affixed from the outside eaves of their cottage each year and lovely it looks. In that neck of the woods the wood pigeon is still widely known as the ring dove, its old name. These days, with the collared dove so common, the old name could be confusing for some as both refer to the neck markings. I love the lazy summer sound of wood pigeons cooing from shady places.

Sunday morning, raining steadily, the valley taking on the fresh greens of spring time, every primrose open and sparkling with raindrops but lesser celandines and wood anemones closed, their petals sheltering against one another, waiting for the sunshine.

We stood halfway between the weir and a bridge, where shallows on the bend of the stream has the water singing a song over shining stones. If you stand still and listen you can hear the ballad of the stream's beginning way up on Exmoor, of its journeying through farmland, past homesteads, through woods and under bridges. And as it flows swiftly on, by the dipper's nest and a tiny island, it tells of its journey twixt fields, beneath trees to a village and thence to the two big rivers as one of its tributaries, before its water pours into the sea, telling waiting salmon of their origins, to come on home to enjoy the freshwater flow, to spawn.

The stream has passed the otter's holt where an old tree leans reflected in a pool that changes colour with the day and night. A thin mossy branch fallen from an alder passes by. Did the otter watch it go by as we are doing? Will it startle the heron standing fishing down by the bridge? The stream the provider for so many creatures and plants.

Below the weir in a small cavern formed when a stone broke away from the weir structure, a pair of grey wagtails are nesting. They have judged the waters will not rise into the tiny cave, and for sure no one will disturb them in this secluded spot off the beaten track, other than cattle who stand here on hot days, to feel the cooling water on their legs. A lovely place.

*I know so well the ancient track that takes me down to the summer time beach,*
*Bestrewn with seaweeds, lace and wrack, and rock pools where the tide did reach.*
*The sea waves lap upon the shore tasting the sand with tongues so light,*
*As fulmars glide about the cliffs in pristine plumage grey and white.*
*A dog is romping in the surf, its pleasure sounding in its bark,*
*As I walk where pink thrift grows on turf, where black rocks point skywards, so stark.*
*Here shags and cormorants watch the sea, here limpets crawl in dark of night,*
*Tis not a place for the likes of me, when a crescent moon is the only light.*
*My footsteps crunch upon the shells, once countless homes of creatures free,*
*Some shaped like cones, and whorls and bells, tiny denizens of the deep blue sea.*
*Along the path an awkward stile, where drifts of bluebells grace the scene,*
*And on again for half a mile to the waterfall in a cliff ravine.*
*And here a wren's nest deeply hid, amongst the ivy evergreen,*
*Is a mossy cave which lies amid the ferns where a stunted oak does lean.*
*I stand with camera in the spray from the cascade glistening as it falls,*
*To take an image of the day and hearken to the chiff chaff calls.*

*Scent of gorse upon the balmy air, green hairstreak butterflies upon its blooms,*
*What can a body do but stand and stare, where a perfect dragonfly darts and zooms.*
*The guttural kronk of Ravens loudly heard, midst rocks and scree they have their huge*
   *stick nest,*
*Ancient site for an even older bird, wherein Arthur, King of Britain, lies at rest.*

Thoughts on days past, and days to come in the lovely Westcountry.

April morning around 9.30am, the sun up and warming, the sound of a pair of mute swans flying down river adding its magic to the spring day, the sound of powerful wings beating the air. But there was more magic to come.

Along the lane is a row of beech trees and in these wood pigeons have nests, squirrels have dreys. Out from one of the dreys in one tree came a squirrel carrying what looked like a ball. She made her way along a beech branch to an adjoining one linking from the next tree and as she came close one could see she was carrying a baby squirrel. Into the much larger drey of the second tree she went, then out again, back to the first drey, to emerge with another babe in arms which followed the first into the larger home. Out again comes mum, back to the drey and this time she emerged with a bigger youngster. In fact it was all she could do to carry it across the beech branch bridges but she made it, human sighs of relief merging with squirrel sighs as mum no doubt tucked up her youngsters and suckled them to her.

When you see or hear of these moments in the ongoing lives of other creatures, suddenly you feel the kinship that is always there but often needs rekindling. The squirrels building larger homes as the family grows, moving house, leaving the nursery nest behind. In a squirrel's life it is all rapid, the young growing, then off to sort out their own lives, all in the same rapid year, not over several years as in humans. I hope they all survive and live long squirrel lives, part of the woods, part of my garden. Magic!

6am. Dull but light, the dawn chorus already over as birds went about the business of springtime. It is good to observe different times of day even in a well known area for not all creatures are about when the majority of people are. Indeed the opposite is more usual, much of the pleasure of a day emanating from the old trees awakening to a new day. Somehow it renews the spirit, as if the tree dryads smile upon those who walk amongst them soon after dawn.

Pale pink milkmaids along the field edge glow in wait of orange tip butterflies. These are the single variety the beautiful, common wild cuckoo flower or lady's smock. Fairy flower it is also called, a familiar flower of damp Westcountry meadows which also has a double-flower form, 'Flore pleno' growing nearby in considerable numbers.

I used to eat the leaves as a lad. They have a pepper cress-like taste and are pleasant on bread and butter. Not that there was much butter available back then in the days of food rationing, but we lived healthily enough, with fish in the streams, and rabbits in plenty.

Bee-bread was also pleasant, the nectar from the white or Dutch clover giving the plant its local name. You had to pull the flowers from the heads to suck the ends.

Blackthorn blossom has peaked and what a wonderful sight it has been this year, better than I can remember so there should be a lot of sloes to come later. Bullens, pig-in-the-hedge, slon tree and snag bush are but a few of the country names for this magnificent hedge tree, powerful against dark spirits. One of my favourite walking sticks is a blackthorn and it's looked after me for many years.

Young grasshoppers also about, a hot, sunny spring day and we are now in a corner of the rough grassland field just sitting and enjoying. Willow is pleased as it is peaceful and secluded, a good spot. I reckon Meadow Grasshoppers (*Chorthippus parallelus*) are the earliest to be out and about, and the habitat here is just right, flat, grassy and not too dry for these green, interesting insects. The Meadow Grasshopper is a non-flying species different from the other British species. Males are generally smaller than females. The true or short horned grasshoppers differ from crickets in possessing short, thickish antennae instead of long, thread-like ones.

Willow nosed at some brown shield bugs in the grass but did not bother to rouse himself from his comfortable position when they moved out of reach. These are *Picromerus bidens*, an insect with no common English name. As they are found in damp, lush vegetation and are often on the ground I think Meadow shield bug will do, fitting in nicely with the grasshoppers.

Close to where the whitethroats are going to nest are a pair of stonechats, the female very close, chasing and eating insects. The male stays in a small area of bramble, often flying to the topmost sprig, flicking his tail, watching his mate's fly catching antics. Wont be long now before they have eggs which the female will incubate for 13-15 days. The young will leave the nest at around 15-17 days before they are fully fledged, and are fed by both parents. Two broods are common each year and I have known three to be raised.

There was a time when stonechats wintered at this spot, then moved elsewhere to nest but a pair always stays on now, all year round, a treat for nature watchers, what a joy, whitethroats and stonechats in this small sunny spot, observable from a few yards.

Various vetches grow along the bank where we sit. Common and bush vetch and the much scarcer bitter vetch. The latter was used as a vegetable, the tubers eaten as well as being used to flavour whisky. The tubers taste a bit chestnutty, the plants hung to dry in bundles to preserve them for later use.

A bee pollinated plant, as are most vetches, the insect feeding on nectar within the flower and picking up the pollen on its underside as it does so.

Bitter vetch is a short, delicate plant, the various vetches being members of the pea family, and including the broad bean so many of us enjoy with a roast dinner.

A kestrel suddenly appears overhead, hovering for a while then drifting on the slightest of breezes, to repeat this seemingly leisurely method of flight until she reaches the woods, to be lost amongst the tree tops. A lovely falcon recognisable from her all brown plumage as a female, the male having a grey head and tail with a black tip. Two days previously I saw a female kestrel perched on the edge of a crow's nest so possibly she is taking up breeding residence there. Falcons do not build their own nests but use the former nests of other species, or in some cases nest on the ground or on stone ledges.

The smaller birds take no notice of her. She is after small mammals, even large insects, and there's plenty of both about. Even as we sit we can hear the squeaking of mice or voles all around in the long grass. Out of sight yet close by us they move along their tiny runways as part of the grassland ecosystem. Ansome!

But let's up and continue our stroll, more tomorrow.

Nature's calendar of perpetual motion has so swiftly flicked by lesser celandines and wood anemones, as primroses, violets and bluebells gave way to June's summer of high grasses flowering unobtrusively. The year's first fledglings of many a bird species are out and about learning how to live and survive. All is movement, sound and colour.

Swallows are feeding young in the old railway subway twixt field and saltings, a tunnel they use each summer, the adults zooming amidst the swirling, swarming insects going about their business whilst forming a living larder for the birds.

Across the field at the wood edge four foxes amble across our vision. The vixen who lives here is out with her cubs. She had them early this year as I saw cubs out on May Day. We watch the little red convoy pass the bramble brake hiding the shelduck's nest without pause, to disappear along a stony track amongst trees laden with blossom. What a hawthorn year it is hereabouts, a splendid sight and scent making up for last summer's less zestful blossoming.

Most of the hawthorns here are the common variety but a few trees in the wood are different. Two are Midland Hawthorn I am sure, and another by the lane has lovely rich pink blossom.

Hairy tare is in bloom along the grassy path, a small vetch with pale lilac, almost white flowers. Its small hairy pods usually contain two seeds. The vetches are members of the pea family, flowers of spring and summer. I see common, tufted and bush vetch all in flower now, a very pretty world. I like tufted vetch in the garden where it grows in one corner but it was once seen as a weed in agriculture where it grew commonly amongst wheat, barley and oats.

Over to Dartmoor to look at old stamping grounds at Crownhill Down, a fascinating wildlife area and important to the overall ecology of the moor. It is about 2-3 miles from Lutton with Hooksbury Wood at its western foot, all good walking country with a number of clay pits about.

Meadow pipits feeding young, a skylark singing and a hunting male kestrel added to the day. Two kronking ravens perching by an old carcase, no not me, had us detour so as not to disturb their lunch.

Oddly as it may seem skylarks gave their name to the lovely Drizzlecombe on Dartmoor, the old local name being Thrushel Combe, meaning skylark valley. Some suggest early mappers of the area misunderstood the local pronunciation of thrushel, for drizzle. Where do these hard of hearing people come from? Us local folk baint that difficult to understand even if us do harden up a bit of 'th' to sound like a 'd'. My maternal grandfather called a thrush a drish I must admit, but twad'n hard to gnaw what ee meant, easier than gladdy for a yellowhammer.

As for yellowhammers I added the species to my breeding birds survey a couple of days ago. The nest was close to the ground in a hedge of dense hawthorn. This would have been a first clutch for the year, second clutches often occurring in July. The female incubates the eggs watched over by her mate, then both adults feed the young. Both incubation and fledging take about two weeks each. Yellowhammers eat insects and larvae, spiders, worms, seeds from a variety of plants, corn gleanings, buds and such.

The yellowhammer is a bunting, the male strikingly yellow with a red-brown rump. Females and young are more heavily streaked and browner but easily recognisable as yellowhammers.

Very dull day. May was rather peculiar really, lots of rain and chilly until the month end. We were over in yellow wagtail country along a glowing green tunnel of a lane heavy with the scent of hawthorn blossom. It is a jack-by-the-hedge year. I've never seen the plant, more widely known as garlic mustard, in such abundance as this year. As cuckoo flower or milkmaids also did well then the orange tip butterfly will have found plentiful food plants and we can look forward hopefully to next year being a good year for them if their June and July larva do well. Safe hibernation in the pupal stage will be critical and they often prefer to over-winter on nearby twigs rather than on the actual food plants.

Look for the butterflies on garlic mustard, their closed wings having a scattered mingling of black and yellow scales which gives an optical illusion of being green. This remarkable camouflage is one of the best in the butterfly world. Indeed it is almost a shock when a male opens his wings and we are presented with the wonderful orange tips which give it is English name. I grow jack-by-the-hedge in the garden so am visited by the insect.

The orange tip caterpillar is green on the back shading into white along the sides, the undersides being dark green. The body is finely spotted with black. There is only one generation a year, the eggs laid singly in young flower heads and hatching in about one week. A fine May and June is thus a critical part of this lovely butterfly's life cycle, as is the non cutting down of its food plants as it eats up to the pupal stage.

High in the woods a lesser spotted woodpecker was busy in an oak, taking insects. A scarce and very small bird it has nevertheless been in this particular area for years as have the great spotted and green woodpeckers. Two years ago the lesser spotted nested in an alder tree at this wood edge by the stream. I found it in sycamore another year no more than 10ft off the ground. It took us an hour of solid and careful looking to suddenly espy a female going into a circular nest hole in an oak close to the one in which her mate was feeding.

We had been looking high but this nest hole was a surprisingly low one no more than 2ft (60cms) from the ground. The oak had fallen long ago but had lodged firmly into the next so was merely at an angle from vertical and thick with moss.

4-6 white eggs are laid, incubated by both adults for 12 days. The young are tended by both parents, on insects, for 18-20 days and what a sight a family of lesser spotted woodpeckers is, high in summer trees, not easy to watch but well worth every minute.

The woods here are on a valley side with pasture fields, the farming landowner giving me free rein to explore. More woods follow along a whole series of valleys for several miles, providing some of the best nature watching in the Westcountry.

A faint drumming sound indicates one of the woodpeckers rattling its little bill on a tree branch. The great spotted drums louder, whereas the green rarely drums.

On the way home we found nuthatches nesting, a day of tree holes and powerfully beaked birds, of trout in the stream, and a bullhead or two, a lovely walk.

What a week of sightings! The good old Westcountry turns up trumps as ever. By the Taw River a cormorant dives into the half tide depths to emerge on the surface with a large flounder. Its attempts to swallow its catch while swimming attract the attention of a greater black-backed gull who swoops down upon the cormorant. A strange but brief tug of war ensues, the cormorant losing its breakfast, the large gull flying to a mud flat pursued by a herring gull also trying to snatch the fish. However the larger gull is having none of that and taking the still wriggling flounder to land it kills it with a few powerful blows, then eventually eats it.

Meantime the cormorant continues its dives further down stream. With plundering, piratical gulls about one wonders how often the actual fishers of the old river lose their catches to the exploiters, the opportunists ready to dive in and hopefully take what is literally up for grabs.

Then along the river bank above the saltings creeks proud mum and dad shelduck followed by a convoy of downy chicks, nine of them piping away. They had emerged from the dense brambles below the woods and were taking their first journey into what is a beautiful but hazardous world when you are a duckling. It is lovely to hear the laughing sound of adult shelduck, as if they are sharing some humorous conversation, or just happy. No doubt about this little group, the pride of the two parents oozing from them as they waddled positively towards the river, mum in front, dad as back marker. Then they all sit down on the grass sward high above the water, to just rest and watch the river and the world go by.

The trail an absolute picture of summertime, hawthorn flanking both sides of our walk and hawkbit a blaze of yellow beneath. We had seen several slow worms out in the sun, lovely silvery bronze, some a foot long. These legless lizards are quite harmless unless you are a slug of course, for they eat a lot of those. I found two in the garden yesterday so I hope they will have young in late summer. I call them 'ours' as we have always had slow worms about and they have been known to live over 50 years! From 6-12 young are usual.

Our slow worms are close relatives of the much larger glass lizard, also legless, which lives in Europe, not in Britain. I still differentiate twixt the two as our wildlife is different, just as our peoples are. And our Field Guides come to think of it! Britain & Europe. I wonder when the powers that be will start making silly rules about that?

The stinking hellebore which grows at the western edge of our woods is over now. It is an interesting plant and aptly named when at a certain stage. Phew! But attractive it is as a plant which flowers in early spring with green blooms edged in a rusty red. We searched the next much bigger wood for it, finding it in just one area, again at the western edge. A wildflower which likes to watch the sunset maybe, or feel the last of the day.

Male and female orange tips have been running the gauntlet of speckled woods, the latter very territorial, seemingly enjoying the sunshine yet immediately darting at any intruders. I've noticed how the orange tips swing to one side if they see the speckled woods in time, dodging around or up and over.

Found eyebright in the garden while I was tidying up the lawn edges. Lovely little flower it is and also known as bird's eye, fairy flax, rock rue and peewits. It was used by herbalists in bread, broths and table beer as well as being applied externally for the eyes. Today an extract made from eyebright and the herb golden seal is still used as an eye lotion so the old Doctrine of Signature theory, that certain plants, because of their appearance or characteristics, cure particular ailments, is not all eye-wash.

I used a concoction I made up myself from eyebright in the 30 years I looked after sick and injured wild animals, if they had eye problems. The water I used was from the old Dripping Well near my home, known to be a healing well. The solution I made up worked very well, ridding many birds and other animals of eye problems. This particular eyebright is *Euphrasia nemorosa*, a common species of some 25 species in Britain. They are semi-parasites which grow best where their roots are attached to other plants such as clovers and plantains. The term parasite should not be a stigma in the wild for there is good reason for them and they simply need to be better understood. Sadly we have allowed the word to be used in derogatory fashion for certain human behaviour, an error of judgement unhelpful to certain plants even though we have a dictionary meaning to support users. There tis.

My pal the male blackbird, dad of the two friendly youngsters, followed me about whilst lawn edging. The pleasant task produced an afternoon snack for the bird who kept darting in whilst saying 'chupp-chupp' in quiet tone, as many members of the thrush family do.

Stream chattering over shiny stones, a bullhead darting for cover beneath a bank overhang as grey wagtail parents take food to their young soon to fledge. On the bank a group of last year's teasels are covered with spider gossamer but this year's are well on and vibrantly green, those from last year a dull chocolate brown.

A golden ringed dragonfly in gracefully busy flight suddenly plunged into the slower moving water flowing beneath alder trees. It is a hot day, the large insect probably cooling off for this plunge diving behaviour is not uncommon in the species. Females are usually about 10mm. I find they do well in the Westcountry probably because they may be found in a mix of habitats from slow to fast moving waterways with silt, gravel or stony beds.

Females of the species will lay eggs into the stream bed in a sort of pogo-stick style, jerking their long ovipositor as they do so. Depending on the stream temperature larvae may develop underwater from 2-5 years yet the insect, once it is on the wing, lives but a matter of weeks. The black and gold banded dragonfly is easily recognisable and not difficult to observe or photograph.

Look for it along waterways. Once found you may sit and watch it patrolling through the day, a superb insect to share an hour or two with. Remember the ovipositor is not a sting and dragonflies and damselflies do not sting or bite us, our pets or livestock. The old names of horse stingers and devil's darning needles are mythical misnomers with no foundation in fact. The golden ringed is often found living alongside other species so we will stay by the water this week.

Sat with Tom Thumb and had Eggs & Bacon all about, a couple of days ago. I was in a field leaning against a good old grassy bank with early foxgloves and hawthorn which had changed its raiment from scented blossom to green haws, preparing its larder for birds and other wild creatures come September.

Tom Thumb and Eggs and Bacon, country names for the yellow flowered trefoils of some of the pea family members, cheery flowers and this particular one, bird's foot trefoil. It is the claw-like appearance of its seed pods which suggest a bird's foot and it is so good to find wildflowers which remain widespread and abundant.

It was a yellow moment, gold lights in the sky way off in the distance and a yellow hammer singing away on a telegraph wire showing where a country road lies over the hedge. His mate will either be on eggs or sorting out their nestling's tea for it was that time of day. Willow snoozed, one eye occasionally checking out the fieldscape, his butterfly ears lifting at any odd sounds.

Down by the river grows our commonest native iris, yellow flag. Widespread in marshes and by fresh water its lovely yellow flowers are large and richly coloured, giving a sunny look to the dullest summer day. I always go out of my way to see it close to for it truly is a most delightful sight. Today common blue damselflies hover and zoom about the iris flowers, some recently emerged and still pulsing the life fluid into their transparent wings. A typical 'summer' species it can be found from May and well into September in the Westcountry I find. With its liking for open areas it is not a difficult insect to observe and well worth watching.

A bit of tit for tat in the garden. Rascal the tabby who has adopted us often basks in the sun on top-shed's flat roof, a spot also favoured by the resident blackbirds. This morning two blackbirds ate his cooked chicken while he was on the prowl elsewhere, away from the spot he likes us to leave his dish. Rascal likes to eat out so to speak and as I write he is on his armchair in the greenhouse having a catnap. Just as well I witnessed the incident or I'd have thought he'd had his meal.

The pair of goldcrests are feeding their young high in one of our conifers, a 3 tier nesting tree with collared doves on the 'first floor', then wood pigeons, and above them the goldcrests. It works well for when a magpie comes seeking eggs or young, usually someone is 'in' and in seconds the nest site occupants are chasing it away.

I found goldcrests nesting in a holly tree one summer and was able to watch both adults building the nest, the male as busy as his mate though I've known that to vary considerably in that on rare occasions the male may spend more time accompanying his mate or watching their territory.

Holly trees are not often mentioned as nesting habitat for birds yet they are frequently used. It depends a lot on their location and if they are in dense broadleaved woodland amongst, say, oaks and hazel, then they provide useful and protective shelter. Holly is widespread and plentiful in woodland in the Westcountry and is a good tree to have about. Near my home is a strikingly lovely golden leaved holly which cheers the dullest days throughout the year, and brightens the sunnier days.

It is a wonderful time of year as long as there's water enough for all so once again I put out a plea for more fresh water in the garden folks. Just a couple of days ago I dared suggest to near neighbours, both of whom have bird baths that they'd be better with water in them. Dearie me! One said his did when it rained, the other, the birds come in on his seed beds. Why have a bird bath? Says I. It turns out that it is part of the 'design' of the garden, not meant to be functional at all.

As it was the blue tits were cleaning the designer gardener's roses of aphids. We watched them doing it. Then they went into my garden for a well earned drink. And what garden designer would put in a bird bath to stay empty? None.

Still, you never know, a timely prompt works wonders sometimes and as it happened it rained hard for the first time for days a few hours later. Somebody heard!

On Dartmoor, in a very well known woodland, lives the lesser stag beetle. We weren't looking for it but found 17 in all, once we found the first. They are black, oblong and very flat with parallel sides. They varied slightly in size but the one I measured was 30mm. Good to see old trees and rotten wood left lying about on the ground, bad news to remove that and tidy up. Though it was a pleasant day I found the adult beetles to be very slow and ponderous as they wandered about on their business.

Useful tip. I mark my walking stick at 6ins intervals from the bottom up. It is handy when you want to obtain rough measurements of things seen.

Considerable subsidence has occurred at the bottom of the woods behind our place. As the 'bottom' is also the top of a sheer 'cliff' drop of 20-30ft in places the lower path is no longer negotiable. Not that it's a public path, that's safely at the top and middle of the woods, but it was a path frequented by locals and youngsters at play. I went quite gingerly along what is left of it and found an interesting wildlife increase due to the lack of regular disturbance. Quite a few low and ground nesting birds were busy feeding young including willow warblers and chiff chaffs, whilst foxgloves had appeared along one landfall area.

What intrigued me most was the close nesting of two pairs of chiff chaffs, the nest separated by only 10ft (3m) of chasm. The fall of stones and soil may have given the necessary impression of well divided territories that suited the birds for they were all busy about the business of catching insects for their nestlings. Both willow warblers and chiff chaffs take about 2 weeks to incubate eggs and a further 2 weeks for the young to leave the nest. In the main, the smaller the bird the shorter the incubation and fledging period.

Looking up over the slope I realised I was more or less beneath our property so a few more landslips and we may be living in the field with a new view and all.

Also found long-tailed tits nesting in an alder tree, the lovely camouflaged nest barely visible against the stem. In fact had I not watched the birds back I would have walked by not noticing the nest at all. What amazing skills goes into the making of many a bird's nest.

More brown trout than I've seen for a long time, a pleasure along a favourite stream also sparkling with damselfly colours of blue, red and green. Occasionally a trout would rise to take a fly, then a splash and back again. It was a dull day after several hot, sunny days, the smell of rain vying with that of recently spread manure, though the rain had not yet fallen.

I once read somewhere that brandy is a good reviver of trout that are feeling faint! True. But what sort of reasons that the fish should be given brandy at all was not stated.

Pollution and water abstraction have done considerable harm to waterways and therefore to the creatures and plants inhabiting them. Flow levels at some streams are worryingly low and one hopes there will be no serious drought situations.

But today as we walked the high grass and buttercup bank the water flowed clear as crystal. One trout, a really large character seemed to follow us for a while before flashing away downstream at speed.

At Moorhen Bend as I always call it, a grass snake slid off the bank, swimming across to the other side, then up and in amongst nettles which were easily 6ft tall, the flowers very pinkish-purple.

Grass snakes often lie cooling off in water on hot days. We had one living with us in pampas grass, by one of our ponds a few years ago. It was a large snake who got quite used to us being about and would lie over the pond weeds watching us with that mesmerising way snakes have. Finding a clutch of snake eggs can be a bit disconcerting but of course the grass snake is quite harmless to us, only the adder being venomous.

'Kwark, kwark', the gentle croak of a toad showed me what Rascal the cat was staring at so intently. I held my hand down and after a few seconds it came to nudge my fingers. I feel sure it is 'our' toad that's been around for a few years now though I haven't seen it for many weeks. Anyway it was in the favourite toad spot by the honeysuckle and clematis arch so received a warm welcome. It used to come out to sit beside me if I sat in the garden of an evening so I must try that again.

Slow worms, too, with about half a dozen golden and striped young, live beneath stones by top pond so they will be keeping slugs in check.

Have put in a new water-to-land log in top pond as the newts are very active at present. They will want to leave the water at some stage and appreciate a 'bridge' to use. A wren uses it to catch insects from and to have a quick dip and occasionally a wasp will perch for a drink which is always interesting to watch.

The wasps have a nest in the bank and from the black triangle on their abdomen these are *Vespula vulgaris*, not *V. germanica* which has a diamond mark. Both are known as the common wasp and as they have the same habits, to know which is which one needs to observe the different markings. They are no problem if left to themselves but it is as well to remember the females of all wasps have stings.

Hornets are nesting in a hollow ash tree some 200 yards from home, in the woods which adjoin our place. They are docile wasps but our largest and quite rare nowadays.

Sandhoppers on the beach, the small jumping crustaceans on the seaweed tideline. They are relatives of sand shrimps and quite common where beaches have not been regularly 'combed' by machines in this silly over-tidy world.

We watched a pair of rock pipits catching these and various insects for their family of four young in a nest about three feet from the beach floor, in a crevice curtained by sea campion. Somehow this species does seem to find what we would term pretty nest sites, even in rugged cliff areas.

This nest is adorned with white feathers and is well placed above the tideline. Quite often nests are difficult to observe as due to awkward terrain the adults are not always easy to watch back even when feeding young. I found rock pipits nesting in an old wartime concrete lookout on the Devon coast for several years but human misuse of the site put an end to their peace and the birds moved home.

Sometimes where there is a lot of vegetation about the nest site the trained eye can pick out flattened herbage telling of the constant to and fro of the adults. Two broods are common but I believe the situation we watched was a first brood of the year.

I have known rock pipits to be feeding young in all months from April to August inclusive.

They are not so well known as meadow pipits, and are larger but slender looking and have darker legs than other pipits. In autumn and winter its plumage is much greyer. Look for this lovely bird around the coast throughout the year. Meadow pipits are also all year round residents whereas the tree pipit is a summer, April to September visitor.

Chilly breeze for midsummer but it was early morning. I pulled my tie knot a little tighter to keep warm and followed Willow amongst the trees. Cow Wheat in bloom, a pretty, low growing yellow flower found in a few oak woodland areas particularly around the coast I notice, and up on the moors. A close look shows deep yellow in the mouth with pale yellow outside, which is almost white. This is common cow wheat, there being a field cow wheat as well. An old name for the common is Hen Penny, and 'Flour' was once made from it which was said to help women have male babies.

I know it in association with the heath fritillary butterfly, and it usually grows in company with wood rush and wood sorrel.

If you believe in Fairies you'd have had quite a jolt from where a spring issues from amongst mossy stones and ferns, several aeshnae dragonflies flew or perched, their shining wings catching sunlight entering the woods in beams. What with the sunbeams flickering through the moving leaves and branches the scene was magical. Shades of Cottingley and all that.

Hard fern flourishing everywhere, like green- toothed combs and common in the Westcountry. It is a beautiful fern with a neat, compact habit and richly dark green, well named as the fronds have a harder feel than most ferns. The fronds that bear spores are quite distinct from those that do not, the fertile fronds standing erect in the centre of the tuft, and twice the length of the barren.

The 'comb' shape also suggests the backbone of a fish hence another old name, herring-bone fern. Look about on a walk and one realises how much the Westcountry's greenery is owed to ferns. Lovely!

Lots of pyramidal and marsh orchids in the rough grasslands the pure pink of the first and the purple of the marsh orchid lovely against the greenery. The pyramidal orchid has a distinct musky odour and it was a pleasure to see so many insects attracted to them. Pollination by insects is an interesting procedure. The modified stamens stick to the tongue of the insect, straightening out during the insects flight and then are pushed directly on to the stigma of the next plant to be visited. Up to 95 per cent of the flowers then produce viable seed. In my home area the pyramidal orchid is actually spreading, doing very well in fact.

The marsh orchids are spreading across a sloping bank of grass and down into the drier part of the marsh. We counted over 200 of them, robust, upright flowers with country names including Adam & Eve, Sweet Willie and Meadow Rocket.

As I write, we could do with some rain but the 'promised' rain shown on TV weather maps seems to be somewhat mythical though Lundy, the Puffin Isle, show clear. It will come no doubt and freshen things up.

Huge swarm of bees in a near neighbours garden, in an apple tree, just after my piece on 'swarms' appeared in the WMN. 'Worth a silver spoon' is a swarm in June. Along came a bee expert and snipped the branch plus swarm into a box and took them off to a new home. A wonderful sight a swarm of healthy bees.

There are several good Field Guides on orchids, most with excellent illustrations to help identification. You could be pleasantly surprised at how many orchids the dear old Westcountry has around and about in wild places, and a few gardens I suspect.

Bees nest in our hedgebank opened up by a badger, a hole the size of a bucket, so someone satisfied its sweet tooth a couple of nights ago. The bees are in and out as usual so life goes on despite the ups and downs.

As a matter of fact it has been a good year hereabouts in the world of bees, the various bumble bees seeming to do well and certainly in good numbers, even though the national picture is said to be gloomy, by English Nature.

Trouble is the evidence of bumble bee declines is largely anecdotal though in south west Germany a 20 years survey shows reason for alarm. In that country severe declines refer to the same species as those which are causing concern in Britain, as well as for some non British Species.

It seems to me that with the bees foraging for pollen as a growth food for their larva, habitat quality is vitally important and it is our own changing ways in the countryside causing food availability problems for bees and other wildlife.

That coupled with the fact that around the planet there are people still testing nuclear bombs and suchlike, is enough to have us worrying about an ever decreasing healthy environment. Whatever filth is discharged from such actions has to go somewhere and I just cannot believe it is not adversely affecting all life, a serious factor in declines everywhere.

Bumble bee abundance, however, will be helped by increased foraging resources, the farmer as ever being a most important link in the chain, providing not only our own food but most of the good wildlife habitats in the countryside.

As I write this our garden is buzzing still, with bees nesting in said hedgebank as well as in a nestbox.

Dull after heavy rain, the trees shining as if newly polished, the patter of raindrops sounding like a million tiny feet roamed all about. Come to think of it they do, and are, but more quietly than raindrops. A red deer stag wanders amongst the trees on the slope above us, on a deer path well used but invisible to us from the wide grassy track we are on. Willow watches the stag out of sight. He isn't one of those dogs who go 'deaf' when they feel like it, then chase off.

Lady's Mantle in full yellow flower, the leaves sparkling, filled with the raindrops. When dew collected on the leaves it was known as celestial water and used by alchemists of medieval times in their experiments to produce gold from common metals. This particular Lady's Mantle is the common *Alchemilla vulgaris*, often abundant in the Westcountry in the wild and in gardens. The English name dedicates the plant to the Virgin Mary, and it has been used to cure women's ailments in the past.

Nice surprise growing with moon daisies along the track side was wild liquorice. I felt I had to get a closer look at it as there are various other vetches about now. This pretty, yellow flowered plant lacks tendrils at its leaf tips and has many flowers together on the stalk. It seems to like being amongst taller vegetation and was a good find. Look for it flowering through July and August. Vetches, members of the pea family all do well in the Westcountry.

Robin had good views of a ruddy shelduck on the Taw River near Barnstaple at the beginning of July. It is unmistakable and the species is an annual visitor here, usually only singles however and often in the company of our common shelduck.

26 Grey herons fishing in a row, as is their right, in their domain. A sight for sore eyes on a summer day with the tidal conditions just right. They were on the sand banks just beyond the saltings, all along the south side of the river as the tide flowed in carrying their fish breakfasts to them. A liquid conveyor belt of tasty meals running the gauntlet of a few birds, the herons legs a stickle as they watched the river with sharp eyes and sharp beaks at the ready.

The heron breeding season is over for the year. Some of these birds were youngsters, the black crowns and predominantly grey necks, the obvious breast stripes and dark bills telling of their youth. If there are no fish about the herons will have a go at frogs, toads, small mammals such as voles and mice, insects and worms, I have seen them take young moorhens, little grebes, ducklings and the like.

Over 100 curlew suddenly back on the mudflats, their evocative burbling calls adding to the essence of the day, the smell of the river on the breeze, the whole zing of well being, of mud on your boots and yielding grass underfoot. The curlews are back early. Well, it was only 7.30am, that's pretty early.

Willow was up ahead nosing at a dead gull. Only just called him off in time, some dogs liking to roll on carrion. Phew, now there is something to avoid if you can. Hardly Chanel or Fabergé. He loped away grinning, scattering dozens of green crabs in the tide creek.

Skylark singing suddenly. Just woke up I expect. Their breeding season often lasts well into September, even though only two clutches is normal per year as far as I know.

It was late in the evening and two of us had been watching a green woodpecker hacking away on an old tree for insects. The bird had been working hard but it surprised me when it laid horizontally along a branch and went to sleep. It was as if the woodpecker had suddenly decided it was time for its rest and off to sleep it went. We could see it clearly, sometimes it stirred momentarily and obviously it was holding on with its claws for it did not slip.

Much of the bird's food is timber boring insect life, and ants are a favourite also. It is noticeable that the bird works the tree mainly from a horizontal position, even on the main trunk.

It is always useful to keep an eye on disused woodpecker holes, disused by the makers that is for other species soon take them over, starlings especially. I have often found bats using them too.

Good, useful birds woodpeckers, feeding on many a pest species of insect and always nesting in trees that are unsound in the heartwood, never a perfectly solid, sound bole.

As with squirrels, when disturbed at a tree woodpeckers will usually keep the trunk between themselves and the observer.

The nuthatches nesting in an oak which has die-back in the crown had decreased the hole size with mud as is usual with the species. We had heard the clear 'pui-pui-pui' whistle before actually sighting the bird. The ones using our nest boxes place a substantial amount of grass and dead leave in as the nest material, a snugly comfortable home. They are quite unmistakable birds in their slate blue and pinkish buff plumage and dark 'mask' through the eye.

Nice drop of rain, the ground needing it, and with no wind it was really pleasant along the stream bank where many butterflies 'hung' in the vegetation. Along this stretch are numerous bullheads, a small fish also known as the Miller's Thumb, essentially a fish of stream bottoms. The large head and gills gives it the English names. It moves about somewhat slowly unless it is darting after prey or is frightened. We are lucky in that two cows wandered into the stream for a drink and the bullheads moved away from their homes, in our direction.

Some say the bullhead is an ugly fish but to my mind it is beautiful, as frogs and toads are, and it is certainly a fish of lovely habitats. No dirty, polluted streams for this creature.

I made a personal study of them for a few years whilst also studying other stream life and found that the male bullhead guards the 'nest' for about a month, always present at the gravel depression where the eggs were deposited. This was observable at night, using my red filtered torch, for bullheads are quite active then.

Also found 3 spined sticklebacks in a clear pool along a leat, the little fish swimming amongst the stems of water plants close to a patch of Himalayan Balsam. The tall pink flowered plant growing on the footpath side of the stream hides the pool nicely so it remains undisturbed and relatively safe. From the opposite 'non-public' bank all can be seen including blue tailed damselflies. A good place to sit. I've been coming here since I was eight or nine so it is a home from home. So many sketches and photos taken here over the years, the bullheads must know me well.

Several Great Pond Snails where the leat moves slowly away from the weir pool. We had been watching bullheads with the trusty old red torch and to see down into the glowing water is rather magical. The species is quite common and seems to like the Westcountry.

Most snails are relatively easy to identify if the adults are examined and species are usually abundant where they occur.

It was an interesting evening as just along from us on the other side of a clump of Himalayan Balsam, a fox came down to the water to drink, so close you could hear its tongue lapping the water. Numerous moths flew about but at night it is almost impossible to identify them unless you get lucky and they perch in the torch light. I don't go in for trapping and releasing.

Bullheads are quite spiny fish their fins looking large as they move about on their nocturnal forays, both these aspects of their lives helping them to avoid predators. By day they usually remain hidden under stones or in crevices in the stream bank. Look for them in gravely or stony waterways with clear, clean water.

Our freshwater bullhead is also known as the Miller's Thumb from the fact that millers thumb became flattened at the top from testing the quality of the flour they were milling.

We may well find a different species of bullhead in seaside rock pools as there are three marine species, two of which are relatively common.

Sighting of the evening was a largish eel in the weir pool. To think it was born in the Sargasso Sea and had crossed the Atlantic to be here for a few years in a peaceful little Westcountry backwater. And here was I considering the long walk home of all of three miles!

Moonlight from a half moon sliding softly between high branches and leaves was all the light we needed along the lane which stretched before and behind us, a grey path twixt dark shadows. The magpie nest is a dark smudge and further on is another showing where the bee swarm is sleeping in peace. It is muggy, the breeze off the river so slight upon ones face it accentuates rather than eases the hot night feeling. We need rain, some serious rain, the ground is hard, the trees and shrubs thirsty.

Rabbits bound away in the bramble shadows where they have runs into the dense vegetation. Here they do no harm whatsoever, the area not a crop situation. In fact their grazing is a good 'management' for the site has more wildflower species than it might without their presence.

There is a sort of warren situation here, dictated by the availability of easy burrowing ground which in itself will limit the number of rabbits occupying the area. Further down river where there are sand hills the rabbit population have it easy for burrowing and do not form warrens, but spread out. Individuals there occupy undefended ranges which tend to overlap with others. At such a site if the population increases the rabbits dig more burrows, any competition then being for food, as demands rise.

However, predation is high, mainly by buzzards and foxes, though in my home area a lot of rabbits are still taken by man, for food. Rabbit pies and rabbit stews remain popular fare with very little beating them for taste and I know at least one fellow whose dog catches all its own food. "Never have to buy meat", he chuckles when we meet occasionally in woods and lanes, "or fish come to that."

Hedgehog with four young in tow by the Sanctuary top hedge, a lovely summer evening sight, more so in that we have not seen many about lately.

They all trundled beneath an old fallen tree which forms a 'cave' curtained by grasses and wood avens. Though largely nocturnal a hedgehog in secluded habitat such as this will commonly forage by day for insects and their larvae, snails, slugs and earthworms. They are partial to fruit, ground nesting birds eggs, and I've seen one or two have a go at lizards.

The family is well grown so should have ample time to fatten up for winter hibernation come October. The main hunting senses are those of smell and hearing, rather than sight.

Down in our marsh field hemp agrimony is growing, looking red and mauve in the evening sunlight. I knew it as raspberries and cream as a lad and here in the rich, undrained soil it reaches 4ft in height. A southern hawker dragonfly was perched on one of the downy leaves, cleaning its eyes with its front two legs, its wings glistening. It may well roost here all night.

The river here is low. We need some serious rain. So many trees and shrubs with leaves dark brown and curling up in shrivelled fashion. The deer wallow site is a baked mud basin at present and feels like rock. The sky goes dark and brooding but there is not hint of rain in the air. Even the thunderstorm we had came to a flash, bang and no water event. But what static. Little blue lights on the wire by a gate, and the old beard actually tingling! But the rain will soon come.

Half a dozen dragonflies appear, perching on the hemp agrimony plants so it looks like a night roost site close to the water has been established.

A woman was picking sea lavender out on the salt marshes. It grows in bluish-purple patches hereabouts, blooming from July into the autumn, and is not uncommon. She realised Willow and I were watching and came over.

"I make flower decorations with this plant. Its colour lasts for ages" she said. "And there's so much of it, and I'll collect some of those teasels later, they look lovely in my stone grate fireplace".

Well there you go. I've seen teasels as decorations used many times but sea lavender was a new one on me, and a very pretty flower. The woman said her hearth was a picture with masses of fir cones too, so she feels as if she is out in the country in her urban apartment.

She said the creek running parallel with the river was alive with small crabs and tiny fish which several herons were enjoying when she arrived. Out on the sand banks a dozen cormorants stood with gulls and curlew, the latter building up in numbers now, adding their lovely burbling calls to the river sounds.

It is a harsh world, the tidal areas, be they seashore or estuary yet life abounds here amongst a multitude of conditions. Light, water, oxygen and minerals aplenty with the twice daily tides varying in height, dictating the boundaries of the shore line.

Sea Purslane was common along a creek edge. 'Daughter of the sea' it is known as, a species covered by most high tides. Its creeping stems root in the mud and the whole plant has a 'floury' look about it. Look now and until

September for the minute green flowers. And do watch out for your safety in tidal areas, remember just the mud alone can be dangerous. Be safe not sorry!

These are always 'firsts' in the world of nature even if, like me, you've been around awhile. Thus when I saw what looked like drops of blood, or old ketchup, on some willow leaves I must admit to being puzzled. Closer inspection said 'galls' of some kind so home to the books and there they are, the galls of a sawfly called *Pontania vesicator*. Evidently they are the only sawfly species which make leaf galls and these I had found were typical, broad bean shaped and on what I call 'violet willow' which I'd planted with scarlet willow years ago by a river. 'Northern Britain' says my book on the subject so the little sawfly has moved to the Westcountry from up North. Maybe it arrived on the willows I bought. It seems sawfly species are restricted to a separate species or group of willows but again there are always exceptions to the rules and in nature, a great deal of adapting is done, usually of necessity.

There are quite a few sawfly species about, the name derived from the female's ovipositor having two saw-like structures with which she embeds her eggs in plant tissues. The larvae often look like those of butterflies and moths. Life for the adults is short, the males dying a few hours after mating.

Those sawflies which bore into wood are known as wood wasps and that includes the Giant Wood Wasp, often known as the Horntail, from its ovipositor, which is not a sting

Ah well, we learn something new every day. Now I must keep an eye out for the little black and yellow sawfly that left the tell tale galls, so to speak.

Interesting subject plant galls, with Blandford Press doing a very good book on the subject, in colour.

Beechmast along the lane, a favourite food of certain birds, especially the finches. It is in the autumn and winter of good mast years that flocks of these birds feed day after day on the ground in beech woods and anywhere the beeches are found, pecking busily at the nuts. Closed canopy beech woods do not have many breeding birds but the more open woods usually have good shrub layers providing food, shelter and nesting areas for various warblers, finches and thrushes which of course includes blackbirds and robins.

Insects and invertebrates of beech woods are many with some 50 or so of the larger moths living on beech. The commonest of these are the vapourer moth, winter moth, grey dagger and November moth I find and of the rarer species the lovely merveille-du-jour lives amongst the beeches at the Sanctuary here.

We had a cock merlin there recently, a surprise really as I have never thought of the valley as 'merlin country', though there is some high moorland within half a mile or so. I have deliberately let the marsh field do what it likes so it is a real patch of wilderness sheltered by steep woods so could attract almost any species. The merlin visited several perches about the place including a standing stone of pink quartz. I think it is quartz. There is a smaller one nearby, probably pintz!

The little falcon was about for over an hour. In August that might mean the bird had moved down from Exmoor following the breeding season and was enjoying a respite in our more sheltered site. Often they will be found around the coast in Autumn and Winter, where weather conditions are more friendly. We certainly enjoyed its company and hopefully it may remain about.

Wonderful year for hornets. Several readers getting in touch to ask about them and none wanting not to have them around which is really good. Odd thing about hornets though is their tendency to come to lights at night, more of a moth thing than a wasp. Big, rather awesome insects they are nevertheless quite docile and I have never had problems with them. Shall we say they react kindly to being left to their own devices, but then so do most creatures come to that.

Hornets have certainly been getting rather rare so to have a really good year is cheering, declines across the board being a depressing thing. I see from past notes they did well in this neck of the woods during 1978-79 and I see Edward Step regarded it as, "not among common insects today", way back in 1932. If I had to have a list of my Top 10 favourite insects the Hornet would be on it, a lovely creature, magnificent insect. Ansome!

Though hornets will nest in the same location for a number of years I have never known them use the previous year's nest. The queen over-winters in a tree stump or in old wood then usually founds her nest nearby. Hornets nests are pale ochre coloured because the building material is old, powdering rotten wood, usually from old oak trees or hardwood beams.

The nest covering always has a finely sculptured surface reminiscent of roof tiles and quite beautiful. There is a wide opening at the bottom as if the nest was cut off horizontally and this allows any debris to fall out as hornets do not carry out their waste.

The best one I have found this year is in a hollow ash tree, just yards from the bee swarm I mentioned previously.

Drove a small herd of cows into a field this morning, Willow instinctively holding his ground to persuade one of them not to bolt by me. The cattle were loose in open grassland, the field gate left open wide by someone, and they would soon have been wandering the Tarka Trail or worse, the saltings. We had come along at the right moment, the ten or a dozen cows not having strayed far beyond their field and they peacefully accepted my drover technique. Or Willow's stern look.

Who would leave a field gate open I can't imagine. It was not even a public right of way field but trails of flattened grass into the bramble area suggested blackberry pickers. All the same if you can open a gate you can shut it again. Straying livestock can come to all kinds of harm.

Anyway, gate secure and good deed for the day done on we went to obtain a photo of a pretty little wildflower we had found beside the path route. It is Red Bartsia, a piratical sort of name 'Red Bart,' which will help me remember it. Fine white hairs give it a dusty look but closer inspection reveals stems of pink flowers all facing the same way and 'snapdragon' looking. It usually blooms from June to August but was late flowering this summer and will bloom through September here I think. It needed the rain on the roots of the grasses from which it extracts water and minerals as a semi parasite.

Red bartsia was once used as a toothache cure, its generic name Odontites, from the Greek word for tooth, odons. Actually its unstalked leaves are toothed so maybe the medicinal use stemmed from a Doctrine of Signatures thing, very popular in days of yore.

The hedgerow is old, gnarled hawthorns beautiful in their aging, a lesson to us to grow as gracefully as we can, to praise life and not fear the next step.

We were standing surrounded by nature's own free health food store and medicine shop. Mugwort with its aromatic scent. I've made a tea from its dried leaves and refreshing it is too, but strong tasting. Put mugwort amongst your clothes to repel moths. You need to today as some of the 'softeners' sold for woollens actually attract moths. Mugwort leaves were also burnt to fumigate sick rooms.

Here along the field edge on the sunny side of the hedge it is growing with yarrow and wild carrot.

Yarrow is one of the great wound herbs and can be identified partly from its feathery leaves and the many flowers which give it an umbellifer appearance though it is one of the daisy family in fact.

Great willowherb is almost over now but bees and hoverflies are about its richly pink flower heads. A couple of elephant hawk-moth caterpillars can be seen near the bottom of one plant but whether they are about to pupate, or feed later tonight, I don't know. It is the time of year for many changes to take place in the world of nature. Apple Pie and Codlins and cream the plant is known as.

Wild Carrot is Kex in Cornwall, and also known as Crow's Nest and Bird's Nest from its drawing together of the umbels when the seed is ripe, resembling a pronounced cup shape. Look for the red coloured flower in the centre which attracts insects. It was used medicinally years ago, the central flower but I don't envy the task of those who collected them.

Sun and cloud, mudflats glistening, water- washed by an ebb tide. Gulls galore, herring, black-headed, greater and lesser black backed, a few 'uncommon' common gulls, everywhere movement and sound.

We had just been watching a kingfisher fly over a hawthorn hedge into the barn owl field, as we call it. There is flood water lying there, the old ditch full, the kingfisher checking it out for fish.

Then the 'tjoo-tjoo-tjoo' of greenshank, such a wild far carrying call and five of these exciting waders flew in to perch on the sandy mud. Seeing five together is not so common on this river, the Taw, so big celebrations later with a muggatee. Saw our first greenshanks this year on August 17th so maybe these are the same birds. At this time of year look for a pale grey wader, with white wedge shaped rump patch extending well forward along the back and a long, very slightly up-curved bill, and yellow-green legs. It is an elegant bird rather like a larger, taller redshank, a much commoner species the latter.

It is known as a passage migrant here but does regularly over-winter in the Westcountry. Look for the greenshank on estuaries and at inland lakes, marshy areas and sewage farms from now through to late March.

Sheer magic here but even more so in Scotland where a few pairs breed. I shall never forget my first nesting greenshanks in a breathtakingly wild and beautiful glen. I shall never go abroad, with so much to see here. There is always a Great Britain in the countryside. The greenshanks ground nest is usually made close to a 'marker' such as a tree stump, rock or fallen branch. Only one brood of young is raised each year.

Below us the river shimmers and glistens like the wings of dragonflies, the purple of heather rich in vibrant colour. A family party of wheatears, five of them, flit after insects as sun and shadows tell of swift moving clouds passing overhead. A few foxgloves on their stems and a few bees hover and search about then swap flowers to search again before moving deep into the heather.

We have just had ten minutes of bliss for an otter had followed Chalk Water down from the Kittuck stone wall, playing with shining stones, then turning the clear water cloudy as it chased a small trout. We had gone up stream to do an evening watch for an article but it was all happening in the daylight, the otter an unexpected yet always hoped for bonus.

The animal had gone on down the waterway and we lost sight of it along the narrow rugged coombe that links Chalk Water to Weir Water, this part of Exmoor one of my favourite places, always providing sightings of heron and green woodpecker and the beautiful green hairstreak butterfly.

We sat drinking in the peace and beauty, the rocks where the otter had clambered out of the water still shining wetly from its passing as it rattled stones in its play. I watched the wet patches gradually disappear on the sun warmed rocks, hearing Willow sigh, dropping his ears back into place for they had been up and listening as he had watched the otter's every move.

Chalk Water actually joins with Weir Water to become Oare Water from here on to Malmsmead with its pretty bridge and ford, a good place to watch dippers, wagtails and maybe have an ice cream.

5th September a magnificent Sunday, no other word for it. Literally millions of spider's webs festooning the bushes, trees and other vegetation across the countryside, the rising sun burning off the dense mist, everywhere shining silver.

On a sand- bank a beached barge had two rather peeved boatmen waiting for the tide and they'd obviously miscalculated the depth of water of the previous one bringing them home. Anglers fishing for plaice added to the misty beauty of the river-scape and downstream from them 10 grey herons and 8 little egrets took small fish in the shallows.

Then a treat as two spotted flycatchers perched in the sunshine along a hawthorn hedge, the grey and white plumage showing up well against the crimson haws. One bird was constantly launching from its perch to take insects from a telegraph pole, one of several across the field. The flycatchers and other summer migrants are fattening up for the long journey south. By the time you read this many thousands will have left and our own daylight hours will have lessened.

In the meander of fresh water across rabbit field was a score or more of red 'lines' on the grasses, common darter dragonflies waiting for the sun to reach them. The emergence of this species has been wonderful hereabouts this year, one of the best I have known.

Willow paused for a drink and a chew of grass by the Dripping Well. He has his favourite grass clumps just as Rascal the tabby does in the garden. Many green acorns down along the pathway, and richly brown beech mast, with here and there squirrels and chaffinches dotted about having breakfast. Still lots of shield bugs, the green species on hazel, no doubt feeding up before hibernating as adult insects. Beautiful.

Squashbugs in the garden on lavender. After rain a strong westerly wind which may well have brought them, winging up river from Braunton Burrows area. These are very handsome insects, bright red with smart black markings quite heraldic in device. *Corizus hyoscyami* it is, the nymphs frequenting rest harrow which grows commonly around our coast. It is a squash bug found almost exclusively round our south west coasts and parts of south-east Ireland. The present generation, which put in an August and September appearance over-winter in moss, juniper and some pine trees. Squashbugs because some species attack squashes and other gourd plants particularly in America.

Common restharrow is a pretty pink flowered plant, low growing and once thought of as a troublesome weed of cultivation where it would 'arrest the harrow' , hence its common name. This was back in the days of horse drawn ploughs and harrows, before tractors.

The leaves if eaten by cattle, tended to taint milk, cheese and butter, giving them a 'cammocky' taste hence the local name cammocks for this member of the pea family. However the underground stems were eaten by children as a great delicacy, tasting of liquorice, hence an alternative country name Wild Liquorice. Rest Harrow flowers from June through September.

There is a Spiny Restharrow which grows in rough grassland. It is pink flowering but grows with more upright, spiny stems.

Lots of Robin's Pincushions about on bramble and wild rose. These strikingly attractive galls add colour to the late summer and autumn hedgerows, already crimson from the haws and rosehips in abundance now. What a beautiful region the Westcountry is at all times. We walked homewards with about 60 goldfinches twittering away just ahead, this years young not showing the scarlet heads of the adults as yet.

Managed to keep an eye on four lapwing nests this summer. As is usual all females laid four eggs and in each case the eggs were placed in an inward facing group with the narrower, pointed ends touching. It is said this is so as to occupy the least possible space but it is more than just that, it is in order that the incubating adult has maximum comfort and provides the greater warmth to them. Imagine the discomfort of a 'seat' with the four larger ends together.

In each case by the way, both adults shared in the incubation for nigh on a month and both shared in caring for the young which take around 40 days to fully fledge.

Male lapwings scrape a number of nest depressions, the female selecting one in which to lay, sometimes lining it with grass and bits of plant material and, usually, placing a small stone between the four eggs, in my experience.

And today I saw a cuckoo flying westwards. That and chiff chaffs singing their September song made for a magical hour or so. The cuckoo was silent of course. Don't know why I say, 'of course' it could call of it wished to I guess, but usually they don't at this migratory stage and probably it was a this years youngster with nothing to call about until next year. Let's hope it makes it back again, and all the swallows, martins, swifts and warblers.

In this neck of the woods the much needed rain was so heavy when it came that quite a lot of birds lost young and nests. Some I was monitoring did not make it, the steep slopes awash for a while, but others did and that is the way of it in the wild, in all life really.

Of the many interesting birds nest records I have been making this summer, some stand out as being unusual, or the parent birds themselves have exhibited behaviour different from the norm. Take the pair of pied wagtails who nested close to a shed which was constantly in use by its wood turner owner. The attraction to the birds would have been the close proximity of a large garden pond with a fountain for wagtails like to have water around.

The nest was in a cavity formed by two large plant pots standing together and was roofed by a row of hanging baskets of flowers. Indeed you could not imagine a prettier home as the trailing plants cascaded and bloomed and four eggs hatched to produce hungry nestlings.

Occasionally, quite frequently in fact the high pitched whine from the wood shed turning lathe could be heard 100 yards away but the birds remained faithful to their choice of nest sites and all was well. However, the unusual behaviour came by way of the adult male as both adults normally feed the nestlings. It was not that he shirked his duties but when the lathe was in use he invariably took food for the young to the female who passed it on to the bairns. She was quite up to feeding them on the nest and on the two days I watched very closely, so was he until the lathe began to scream and whine.

As for recognition of human individuals by birds they certainly do know who is who in familiar territory such as ones garden. Several of the birds who come in to be fed know me and fly over to wait as I stock up food and fresh water for then but if a stranger comes, they take one look and go.

Buff tip moth caterpillars suddenly everywhere in this neck of the woods, North Devon a superb wildlife area still, despite the constant development encroachment and consequent loss or fragmentation of habitat. And I know it is the same generally in the Westcountry, the WMN covering a region that is a delight to nature watch in.

Along the lane this week has been a regular 'caterpillar' of children from the nearby school, 'under elevens' and it is good to hear them go chatting by on their way to the river.

"Look acorns! Put one down Jamie's shirt."

"Ooh! A squirrel right on the path. Look at that jump!"

"Hey Miss, is that a bird house up in the tree?"

"Yes Kyle. A nest box. The birds go in and out of that hole."

"What birds Miss? Blackbirds?"

"No I don't think so. Blue tits do. No not swans Amy. Can you imagine a swan trying to get in that hole?"

"Yes, I can imagine it miss."

The voices fade as the group goes by back gate and all is quiet again. The school children are fortunate to have a place for easy walking and teachers who will take them out regularly. The walk itself will be good for them, some healthy exercise, sunshine and fresh air. If they learn one or two things along the way, all the better.

I've just been corresponding with a youngster doing a GCSE study of the various likely effects of the proposed new Barnstaple downstream bridge. He is obviously very keen and enthusiastic, polite, and knowledgeable. Must cover all the green aspects, he told me. It is good to find young people getting to grips with these issues which one way or another affect every one of us. Bodes well for the future.

North Easterly wind blowing strong and the tide about as low as it gets, but the grasslands just in over from the highest reach of the tides were heaving with grasshoppers on a mid September afternoon. It was lovely to see them, these the common field grasshopper, *Chorthippus brunneus*, a large insect which is very active in hot sunshine. Listen for a series of short chirps from this gregarious grasshopper right into November, sometimes later.

This species is found in a wide range of habitats but prefers dry situations. Where we are standing watching them is a sort of sun-trap twixt woods and river.

We had been watching ground-hoppers, dark brown insects grasshopper-like and found in mossy habitats. Adults and nymphs will be found together more or less across the year for the females lay eggs over a long period. They cannot fly but leap and swim very well. We have one kind living in the garden where moss grows in an area I have left for ivy and periwinkle ground cover.

Surprise bonus, a buzzard, sparrow hawk, kestrel and peregrine all in view at the same time. The peregrine and sparrow hawk had flown by whilst the kestrel and buzzard were keeping to the long rabbit field, the latter hovering close to the long ditch that divides the field from the disused railway embankment.

The embankment is an excellent wildlife habitat, south facing and sunny. Lizards love it there and each summer we go to see the glow- worms light up the night shadows.

Excellent book on grasshoppers. Called "Grasshopper and Allied Insects of Great Britain and Ireland", it is by Marshall and Haes, published by Harley Books. A good book shop will get a copy for you.

A few knot about, with black tailed godwits, a lovely sight as an ebb tide caught the pink lights of sunset, colour rich and changing so swiftly to red. The knot is a wading bird about half way between dunlin and redshank size, with a short, straight beak and short thick looking legs. The winter plumage has a grey fish-scale effect and the underparts are white. In flight a white wing bar is visible, and a whitish rump with fine darker barring.

Today as we watched them the copper colour of breeding plumage was still visible. It is the rather subdued 'nut' call which probably gave them their common English name. Now, on the estuarine habitats knot will eat marine organisms such as crustaceans, annelid worms and molluscs. In the breeding season plant seeds, buds and insects are taken.

In the changing lights the saltmarsh is awash with the yellow centres of sea aster, the petals all having dropped away, a glorious mass of colour stretching away into the distance. Sea aster was commonly taken from the wild to grow in gardens but the showier Michaelmas Daisy, introduced from North America replaced it.

The Sea Aster will be found in flower to the end of September usually, but 'ours' along the Taw River were mostly up and over by the first week in September this year. It is also found on sea cliffs around the Westcountry coast, a pretty wild flower well worth looking out for.

It used to be known as Musk Button, Blue Chamomile and Summer's Farewell. The roots were used as a wound herb and against dropsy and various poisons so a useful plant to have around.

As ever, if you are exploring tidal and coastal areas be especially careful.

Steady rain all day, but nice enough if you don't mind getting wet. With a waterproof somewhere between teal and mallard green, moleskin trousers and a hat with a jays feather in it I felt my plumage and pelage would keep the rain off. Willow a bit hesitant. He did a lot of staring and weighing things up but once we got going he was fine, a good old lad.

Masses of acorns this year. To think last year readers sent me some because it was a poor crop year hereabouts. Seventy of the oaks from those survived by the way folks so they should now become fine trees. I've been looking around at the hundreds of trees we've planted over the years. The field maples are around 8ft tall now, looking splendid and the guelder rose, dogwood and rowan trees have all done well. Their late autumn colours will be a picture, the dogwoods especially, hence the Latin name *Cornus sanguinea*. Of course I planted hundreds of oaks, beeches, chestnuts and a few other species. In the main very few problems have occurred, though deer lunched on one or two, particularly the white poplars.

How glad I am I planted 200 alder buckthorn. All are doing well now, though three didn't take right at the start. Brimstone butterfly trees they are, well, shrubs really, and they love it with the oaks along the wood edges.

Now as November swings into view tree and shrub planting is a good thing for the countryside, the garden, and keeps a body fit. Plant now and see the beauty of your own trees come into leaf. And if no room for a tree, put in a shrub or two, lovely to look at, good for wildlife and years of pleasure.

The pattering of rain and falling acorns, shining green ovals of colour along the wood path lit by weak sunlight. A pretty sight, cheering and speaking of future oaks for surely a few will germinate.

And if you think the days of really good stage acts are losing out to TV I can promise you it is not so in the wild. We were down by an open field and could hear 'laughter' as we approached a gate. Carefully looking over so as to avoid disturbing the jollity, there in the field by the river were six shelduck sat in a row. Directly in front of them two youngish rabbits were gambolling and pirouetting about, occasionally rolling about, as they did so the ducks would utter their laughing calls. It was a lovely sight for any nature lover but for me it conjured up images of a great variety act and its appreciative audience, including us. Ansome!

And at the top of a whippy hazel branch a grey squirrel was watching with one eye, the other on the nearest cob nuts. They, too, have done well this year but whether the old tradition of 'nutting' is still upheld anywhere in the Westcountry I don't know. I believe it was Gladstone who said at 81 years of age he had not eaten a nut of any kind since he was eighteen. Odd sort of thing for him to remember and say, but politicians do have their wise moments I dare say.

Nutting season began on September 14th, the day of the Holy Nut, but I am not sure how long it goes on for. Acorns were traditionally sown on October 15th, for future timber, and it was said one should beware of earthquakes on 17th. Sloes and quinces may be gathered now.

Saturday – an October weekend, so often very beautiful. Fresh Westcountry air to blow away the cobwebs. How about a bracing Dartmoor walk folks, over in Tony Beard Country and Paul Rendell Country?

On the east side of Saddle Tor is a small car park, just off the main Bovey Tracey to Widecombe-in-the-Moor road. Land Ranger Map 191 will set you right, Grid Ref 754764 will be your start and finish point. A bit over 6 miles (10km) this walk, map miles of course. Face Haytor and go uphill from the back of the car park towards the upright bondstone. Go over the hilltop and you will find several old granite quarries. Follow the path that runs by the road, keeping Lower Man to your left and turn between the Tor bosses. A clear path goes down towards the fenced in Haytor Quarries. You will soon find yourself by the granite tramway which you can follow without walking on and damaging it. Now, I can't go into much detail in 300 words but a narrow path will be found to take you to the top of Smallacombe Rocks with glorious views of the Becka Brook Valley. Go on over the summit to bear half left on a path leading to the valley bottom.

Find the Clapper Bridge over Becka Brook and go up the steep path, through a wooden gate and you'll see Greator Rocks from the top. Go on to Houndtor, through the central avenue and half left, to the right side of Greator Rocks. You will find a gateway with an information board and fingerpost. Waymarks from here across the Becka Brook again, through Emsworthy Enclosures, to Saddle Tor and down again to the car park. Beautiful walk, buzzards, ravens, maybe me and the gang!

Acorns everywhere, mostly oak brown now, with a few fresh green ones amongst them. One could exercise the rights of pannage and feed ones pigs very nicely this year. Most of us know about pannage yet it could not have been of widespread importance in this country for every year is not an acorn year. Woodland was more of a bonus to the pig keeper in some years rather than something he or she could rely on annually. People ate acorns too, at times. I believe pannage still exists as a common right in the New Forest though stand to be corrected on this. The main area of pannage was in the Weald, which occupies the greater part of Kent, Surrey and Sussex and a bit of Hampshire. Gilbert White of Selborne wrote so eloquently of his patch and the wildlife, and the Weald yielded the bones of huge dinosaurs not so long ago. Now some of those, the herbivorous species, would have mopped up a few acorns no doubt.

Willow, our collie, is an oddball with acorns. He sniffs one or two, picks one up, cracks it open and drops it back onto the ground. Speeding up natural regeneration of oak trees perhaps, a friend of trees is he.

Bit of a surprise early this morning was eight moorhens all together in a flooded area beneath willow trees. They were just drifting on the water, brought by recent rains, a delightful sight in what is a very interesting green tunnel. In a month or so it will be lit by the sunlight for the leaves will all have fallen. Such changes add to the interest, making nature watching an all year round joy.

Watching the moorhens drift slowly along green tunnel was one of those moments that inspires a painting or two. I called Willow and he followed me in under the trees to be better able to see along the stretch of water. We moved quietly so as not to disturb the birds but someone else had other ideas. From behind us the shrill cries of an alarmed blackbird and a hunting sparrowhawk came loud and the thud at my feet was the blackbird, a male, seeking sanctuary against my boots.

The hawk, thwarted by my presence flew on low along the water channel and eight moorhens dived in unison as the little raptor swept on in search of food.

The moorhens had dived instinctively, soon bobbing up again, each moving off into the tangle of vegetation at the waters edge. The sparrowhawk would not have attempted to take such prey I feel sure, especially in water over a foot deep but it had ruffled a few feathers in its passing. The blackbird pecked at my boot, went 'chuck-chuck', then flew up to a branch to preen and live another day.

I stood with Willow gazing along the water. Just a few swirls of movement showed where the moorhens were deciding to come out into the open again. The blackbird dropped to the ground and yanked a worm out of the soil for its own meal. Beside us a robin sang and a rather tattered speckled wood butterfly alighted in a small patch of sunshine. The hawk incident must have been all over in ten seconds. A moment I'll not forget, just a 'blink' in time and now the blackbird was the predator. The earthworm eaten it flew up and ate a rose hip for desert.

Misty rain sweeping across the landscape, the old tree stump that was a useful summer seat now soaked. Growing from it are small rows of pearl grey fungi not found in the mushroom and toadstool field guides. However, I've watched them emerge each autumn so know they will soon grow larger to become the pink-brown 'Jew's Ear' fungus best known in its mature form.

I trust it is a useful tip for readers interested in fungi identification, to go back regularly to see how the fruiting bodies develop and quickly reach the mature stage shown in most books.

Jew's Ear is common and often does resemble a human ear as it grows, mostly on elder tree dead branches, but not exclusively. It was known as 'Judas Ears' from the belief Judas Iscariot hanged himself on an elder tree, and over the course of time the name was corrupted to Jew's Ear.

It is edible and appears in some of the Chinese restaurant dishes served in Britain though we westerners tend not to eat it so much. Amusingly I was on a fungus foray some while ago when the leader was picking some species to eat. He avoided Jews Ear saying he just did not fancy eating a fungi shaped like a person's ear. Well, some of the shapes he had chosen to eat should have put him off for life one would have thought.

In the woodland grasses where bluebells and celandines grow in spring is a short row of honey fungus. Its appearance here traces the unseen, dead root of a tree. Honey fungus varies in form so again, check shape and habitat carefully to be sure of the species. I've made an error or two identifying fungi and like to sketch and photograph them on site.

Mushrooming in the drizzle, a free feed as part of a pleasant walk, with Willow for company and mallard waddling by the ditch. I could see Willow was staring into a hawthorn, very attentively and that is usually good news for me as he does not miss much. I followed his gaze to a blackbird's nest showing clearly from my crouched, mushroom picking position and was about to dismiss it as disused when I, too, spied the movement that had attracted Willow's attention.

It is that time of year when 'old' nests become larders, for wood mice store hips, haws and other fruits in them. I could see the mouse crouch then leaving the nest it scampered down the hawthorn trunk to disappear in the grass. Well, the rain was coming on harder, so shelter seemed the sensible thing. Willow agreed so with our fungi lunch we trekked homeward.

The wood mouse is also known as the long tailed field mouse. It is an active little mammal that may be seen running and bounding about in a variety of habitats including woods, hedgerows, sand dune areas and gardens. They do not hibernate but may go into a torpid state in cold weather times which helps them survive food shortages, as do their 'larders'.

Breeding begins in March and a female may have up to four litters in a year, of four to five young. With a high mortality rate and a maximum life span of around two years numbers rarely reach proportions that would cause us problems. They are also preyed on by owls, other birds of prey, foxes, stoats, weasels and such. Most wood mice adhere to the same general area so if you see one or two about it's well worth watching the site.

Talk about expression on the faces of animals! Not far from the river near home is a stone wall, a considerable structure, part of an old railway subway no longer used. As you walk down the slope beside it so the top of the wall becomes head height. I had just got to this point, on my way to look at a fresh water marsh area when a squirrel scrabbled onto the flat wall top and we were face to face at about two feet distance.

The little character had a hedge nut in its mouth, front teeth showing, and an astonished look on its face, one of definite incredulity I'd say as it stood up on its hind legs, one paw on its chest. Then, still with the nut firmly grasped it leapt over my head to land in the branches of the tree behind me. My turn to be astonished as I had half expected it to turn and run for it. By the time I'd ducked and turned it was yards away leaping seemingly effortlessly along the swaying branches. What grace and agility they have, gosh if I could throw my body weight around like that, even without a nut in my teeth.

Winter will follow autumn soon, as relentlessly as the incoming tide from the sea, with a mix of cold and mild days to enjoy. In the great outdoors there is always the chance of rare or uncommon sightings but the fun and humour often comes from those every day moments. Willow for instance, drinking the raindrops caught by the leaves of lady's mantle showed how important such water sources must be for wild animals. And the magpie riding across a field on a cow's back this morning at crack of dawn, keeping warm possibly.

The woman at the shop counter, waiting to pay, turned and saw me.

"Oh, you are just the man," she said. "I've bought two jars of horse radish. We love it with a beef roast, but what is it? Where does it come from?"

Two things occurred to me. One, I was glad I am into herbs and their uses but also that we are a trusting lot really aren't we. We pick up jars of all kinds of things and as long as it's off a shop shelf we take it for granted all is well. Yes I know we have to , and it usually is all hunky dory but it's interesting to ponder on.

Horse radish. One of the cruciferae and a perennial from eastern Europe. In my days of having an allotment I tried growing it but it did not do so well. It is the root that provides the popular rather mustard-like condiment. It was once used as a cosmetic to get rid of freckles and keeping a clear complexion.

I told the woman about those uses. "Coo," she said, then to the shop owner. "Mr.Beer's told me about this lovely horse radish and it should be over on that shelf with those lipsticks and eye make-up." And off she sailed.

"Oh yes. What's all this about then? Horse Radish and lipstick? You don't want to go around telling my customers things like that".

I paid up and left. Outside the woman was chatting to another. She pointed as I passed. "Him. He told me you can rub it on your complexion. I shall try it."

Dearie me. Not what I said at all but somewhere a lady covered in horse radish is probably also enjoying a beef dinner.

Pretty little moth about, the Many-Plumed moth, which has grey multi plumed wings. They fly at night from August through the autumn when they then hibernate in ivy, or sheds and barns. In spring they are common wherever honeysuckle grows, the larval foodplant of the species.

Making a list of 'late' blooming plants and 'late' flying insects as we progress into winter we found 30 wildflowers in bloom on October 1st. Two of us also caught and released a brown aeshna dragonfly on the same day, a large hawker. It was a rather splendid male with bright blue eyes and yellow wings.

A few slow worms about, and a very large grass snake by Shearford Lane, Barnstaple, all of 42 inches long. I find the one inch notches on my walking stick very useful indeed.

Wrens have begun using one of our nest boxes as a night roost so no doubt this is happening all over the region. Night roosts of birds keeping warm and in some cases picking up insect food from buildings is becoming more common, wagtails being notable for some very large roosts.

200 crows together on the sand bank by Pottington, Barnstaple was a fine sight as the tide ebbed, and we counted 78 jackdaws going to roost nearby, in trees along the Tarka Trail.

And hedge woundwort still in bloom, lovely, a purple flowered member of the mint family with quite a powerful smell. You will find the nutlet fruits now and through November, in fours located at the base of the calyx. Look alikes include marsh and field woundwort, and betony. They all flower through the autumn so may still be about. Saturday again… off we go to see what's about for next week. Ansome!

To lovely Somerset to talk to 'Down Memory Lane' people who wander down to the village shop each morning for their WMN. An October day with sunshine, the Levels shimmering under a clear blue sky. So many common darter dragonflies along a rhyne it was almost unbelievable even though one knows they are usually the last species on the wing for the year.

Comma and speckled wood butterflies too, and several large whites, all about in the October sunshine. Then a couple of special finds, a medlar tree in a hedgerow, and lots of white deadnettle in full bloom.

The medlar is a lovely tree with a single showy flower which appears in early summer at the end of each short, leafy twig. For centuries the fruit was eaten as a delicacy and believed to be a cure for many ailments. They should not be eaten until over-ripe, a process usually begun by the first frosts. The fruit can be picked and laid out under cover for about two weeks. The fruit can be made into a jelly. It is a yellow-brown colour with a deep hollow at the end, surrounded by large, conspicuous withered sepals.

Here in the wild hedge along with hawthorns the tree was a fine sight but these days it is grown more as an ornamental for its flowers and richly russet autumn leaves. Medlars originated from the Caucasus, or in planning departments. Or is that spelt differently?

In Somerset the White Deadnettle is known as Adam and Eve in the Bower, and I've heard it called Honey Bee in Devon. A beautiful plant with no sting, hence deadnettle. Here in flower in October it was a joy all along the quite roadside. A real beauty.

☙ ✦ ❧

"Have just been across the pond for two weeks holiday."

A near neighbour beamed at me as I was coming home along the lane with Willow. I asked him if he'd got a tent or caravan in the garden, to which he looked very puzzled.

"No. We haven't why? Do you need a tent?" he asked.

My turn to look puzzled. Then it dawned on my little grey cells. Hastings, I thought, this man has been to the USA on holiday, not across 'the pond' at all. I explained my silly error. Well, fancy calling an awesome, magnificent ocean a pond. So I said so.

"But with air travel being what it is today the ocean is getting much smaller in time factor terms you see," says he.

"Getting bigger you mean. Climate change is causing the seas to rise. Serious stuff," I replied.

"Oh that. Lot of twaddle. What are a few feet of water? You wont notice it. Just like a high tide. Reservoirs could do with more water as it is. And some experts say we could have vineyards all over the Westcountry."

Well folks, there's one answer to farm diversification. Grapes.

I walked home, reassured that any surplus water sweeping in over the coast will go straight in our reservoirs and wine will take over from milk. Just imagine, how would you like your coffee? Black or sort of merlot red. Willow rolled on his back when we got in. I think he was laughing.

Well I think the rising of the seas will be a serious matter. Not that our government, or our MPs are showing signs of worry. They'll have moved on. And the new ones wont be to blame. You will hear that well worn phrase, "it is an inherited problem."

Blowing wild, white horses on the river. Pretty name really and we all know those whippy tail like wind blown waves aren't really white horses even if at least one cleverly made TV advert tempts us to think otherwise. Trouble is a lot of the time we see 'sludgy horses' blowing in, and plastic foam, discarded flip-flops and drink can horses. Gosh a recycling company along our 'strand-lines' could make a fortune.

My friend Keith over in Somerset meets a particular horse on his rambles most days and they've become good pals. The noble beast, the horse that is, greets him and that is rather nice I reckon.

"So early in the morning the ploughboy he is seen, all hastening to the stables his horse for to clean. The mane and tail he will comb straight, with chaff and corn he will them bate, and he'll endeavour to plough straight, the brave ploughboy."

An old country song and always sounding best from the old timers who worked the land, somehow. I tried my hand at guiding the plough a few times in my youth and keeping a straight furrow was more thanks to the horse than to me. However I loved to groom horses and chat away to them as I made their coats shine. They got to know your voice and you knew they were glad to see you. I loved it when birds came down and took horsehair for their nests. Must do a "Down Memory Lane" on that.

Willow and I plod on, leaning into the cold east wind, homeward now. A hat passes us by, rolling on its brim. Up ahead a fellow rushes towards us in hot pursuit. Well, cold pursuit. Perhaps it was a hat that 'invented' the wheel.

"God this weather is awful!" The groaning words came from a fellow along the path by the saltings. True, it was stair-rodding with rain and cold with it. But he had on what looked like a very good coat, down past his knees, and a hat, so I told him he looked well protected.

"Oh I know," he said. "But it's a brand new coat and now it'll get soaked through."

I wandered on with Willow. Followers of fashion. I wondered why he hadn't just left the coat home and worn an old one but I guess to look 'right' was the important thing. Poor chap was in the wrong place. A shop doorway in the High Street would have been better.

Willow and I walked on, every so often a great squally gust stopping us in our tracks. Seven grey herons lined up like old men, gaunt and rain-swept, then beside them two mute swans and a little egret, then a huddle of mallard. They all seemed to be watching a flock of over 100 dunlin, the tiny waders feeding away with that rapid, 'stitching' motion they have, probing the mudflats.

The 'Kronk, kronk' of ravens came loud. Dearie me, that'll bring in a letter from the Henry Williamson Society. I looked up, as you do, but the ravens, two of them, were down in the rabbit field sheltering under the hedge of hawthorns. One was feeding on carrion perhaps a dead rabbit. Ravens pair for life, like swans and some other species.

A nice sight. 'Kronk' said the one not feeding and the other moved aside to give it a turn at breakfast. Real mates. Lovely to see that, two magnificent birds of the crow family sharing a meal. Made my day.

A near neighbour was springing about on the lawn of his and his spouses house, hitting the grass with a tennis racquet and making a racket by shouting loudly. His mate of many years watched him, hands clasped in prayer-like posture as he cavorted about.

Some new game? Solitaire Tennis? Or a new gardening technique, healthier than mowing the lawn? The words issuing forth were of a Saturday night in Barum High Street type and not of any scientific terms I recognised. Plucking up courage, hoping I was not about to interrupt an important part of the strange ritual I shouted, "what be ee up to then?"

"Ah, it's you. Good. Can you come in a minute?"

I went into the garden. "There! Look there! My wife is frightened of anything like that."

'It' was a very large toad. He had been attempting to hit a walking toad with said tennis bat. I recalled I'd rescued frogs and pipistrelles for them before in past years.

I picked up friend toad and chatted to it about its new life in our garden, and off I went. Phobias must be responsible for a lot of wildlife mortality. Snakes in particular suffer in this manner. I wonder if other animals have phobias about humans? I imagine they do.

Toad and I sat together for half an hour while it recovered from what must have been a scary time. How it was uninjured I don't know. Obviously the Gods love toads. Well I couldn't promise it a yellow horse drawn caravan or a bright red car but if it stays here it will be safe from Henmanitis and the natural food is plentiful.

I was never good at tennis, soccer, rugby and such. I was a good cricketer though and could run like a stag.

Have you ever thought how badly off we humans are? Compared with most plants and animals other than homo sapiens? I like God very much, a real fond 'like' but if I am ever called to explain my lapses as a human, if I reach the Pearly Gates, I have a list of complaints which will no doubt get me slung out. "Go back and start again, He will say and I shall pop back and see if the WMN will take me on again. Sounds of laughter from Plymouth.

The thing is, what a sense of humour the Great Architect has got. Saw a group of mallard sitting in the sun by the river today, just watching the world go by. In one of the hollow ash trees near our place a tawny owl gazed out from ivy, waiting for the sunset and dinner catching time. Nearby red campion bloomed and winter gnats buzzed about in a sunbeam. A contented lot all of them, well, relatively contented but if some predator 400 times my size suddenly swooped on me I wouldn't know much about it anyway.

But we so-called top of the range thinking creatures have created so many mill- stones to hang about our necks that it is a wonder we can walk. Committed to the system we are and some say it is evolution. Cor!

Anyway I sat on a plank seat near the ducks enjoying enough blue sky to make a sailor's trousers, so it shouldn't have rained. A small flock of house martins whizzed down river, the late ones heading south whilst beside me a red admiral fed on blackberries now a bit squishy. Soon, probably as you read this, it will be fast asleep in hibernation. Nice that. Good luck to it.

Not brass monkey weather exactly but cold enough, as told by the tip of ones nose. We had been waterproofing a hut in a wild wood so expected to see some interesting goings on and were not disappointed. Close by us two nuthatches more or less demolished a pile of peanuts we had placed for all comers, though other species had joined in on the feast.

It had rained on and off but we were well protected by a dense canopy of leaves so had carried on with several tasks that need doing as winter gradually sets in. Down by the river otter signs were everywhere, footprints and spraints in abundance thanks to the mud and a few useful sprainting areas such as a log, a large rock and a small beach formed by accretion on our side of the waterway. Such signs are exciting but do not mean an abundance of otters so much, as an otter or two regularly using the area. That is really good news.

The footprints of an otter are called seals and in wet mud are readily identifiable by the five- toed prints of around medium dog size. Luckily we'd had our share of rain and instead of staying in, it is a good time to go out to explore for tracks and signs. Showery weather is very good, incessant rain will soon wash tracks away.

I know wild otters very well. They are quite different from captive otters in behavioural terms but you can learn a lot from them if you are prepared to spend the time and take whatever weather Mother Nature sends your way. And the beauty of it is you see so many other sightings. Maybe I will get the opportunity to tell you all about that one of these years!

7am. Cold and grey. Much caterwauling from the back garden area, really loud and creepy. Rascal was out and about, and Kate the large tabby and white cat from a few properties distant, plus a 'new' arrival in the area, a jet black fellow. It was he doing the howling, an amusing sound, so loud I thought the 'Beast of Exmoor' was about. Simple solution, door open, out rockets Willow, barking and exit one rapid caterwauled. Opened back gate to give Willow his morning constitutional and there was a fellow dusting himself down.

"B – thing ran through your hedge right into my legs." He grinned ruefully. "Gave me a turn. All black. I fell over."

He was none the worse for the experience and was on his way home from a night shift somewhere. What a start to the day.

Then a pleasant surprise. Perched on the old railway subway wall, which could tell a few stories, was a male black redstart. Almost certainly it will spend its time at the nearest light industry complex on the edge of town as the species often does. There amidst the shelter and relative warmth the bird will find insects through the winter.

A bird of crags and screes, the buildings, concrete blocks and gravel piles of the building supplies firm will have it feeling at home, and there are masses of berries about to augment its invertebrate food.

The bird has the typical red tail of its kind and is otherwise sooty coloured with white wing patch. Females are mainly dark brown. Look for the character-istic tail flicking, 'start' by the way being from 'steart', an old word for tail.

Our summer visiting common redstarts will have left us by now to return again come April.

I still haven't gotten around to patenting the cream cord material with dog footprint pattern all over it. Each time I wear light coloured trousers I meet Tom, the Collie, one of Willow's pals. He has a scout out checking what I am wearing, then he bounds and leaps to kiss my ears which are six feet from the ground. Muddy ground of course. If I'm already muddy and in the old gear we never meet him. Good old Tom.

We were on our way to photograph redshanks as it was sunny and I wanted bright red legs and good reflections in the water of the creek. I have been up the creek for years so I knew my way around, deciding to work from a large tree stump which provides an excellent vantage point since the fallen tree left a gap in the row of oaks and sycamores.

As we neared the spot a grey shape was in view and then a handsome face turned our way. Well, I knew it couldn't be mine so up went the trusty binocular and there was a golden eyed short eared owl nicely perched enjoying the sun's warmth.

I love owls, I think most people do, and to see one in the wild is always exciting. Short and long-eared owls are not common in the Westcountry, tending to be more wintering species but they occasionally breed. I used to find short eared owls in summer on the Somerset Levels during the 1950s and beyond. Wonderful ground nesting birds and what a joy to watch quartering the marshes to find food for their young as the farmers carried on with their work.

At this time of year look for them around coastal and inland marshy sites, perhaps perched on fence posts and telegraph poles during daytime.

Pouring with rain, that lovely tinkling sound of water down the drains and a pattering on the windows. So I'm not going out nature watching, to get soaked through. Instead I shall look around the den and muse a bit. There's Collins 'Complete Bird Book' on a shelf. They never did do one on incomplete birds. A shame that. There's another on 'Secret Sites in Britain'. Well, not secret once the book was published. What a treasure that would be if it had blank pages.

I recall a TV programme where this presenter chappie crawled into a cave and as he came towards the screen he said how he was the first human who'd entered this cave for centuries. Not a word of praise for the camera man or woman who'd gone in first to set it all up. The book on the presenter's exploits is on the shelf, a great sort of explorer who'd done this and that 'first', with photos taken by someone else, to prove it.

I boobed like that once. Did a book with many pictures, 7 or 8 of which were not taken by me. One was by Endymion, another was of me and I didn't take it. I sent a list of the picture credits that weren't mine, and an index of contents. Both were omitted. Guess who got moaned at when the book came out? I also did a very tiny book years ago, more a booklet really. A reviewer wrote about it pleasantly then criticised the fact it was index-less. If it had an index that would have doubled the number of pages. I still have the review.

It is still raining. Must take Willow out. Gosh, the errors I've made, I worry I may be human. Not so ansome!

A letter from a reader in Gloucester reminded me of seeing two sparrowhawks taking jackdaws in flight around the tower of Gloucester Cathedral in the 1960s. The hawks, undoubtedly a mated pair, flew into a flock of these small crows and simultaneously took a 'daw' each with no trouble at all. Such a splendid building, the cathedral, its tower and general affect pleasingly grand.

We had been in the Cotswolds, poking about from Tewkesbury, Deerhurst and down the Severn to Berkeley, then home to Devon, for midsummer as I recall.

The reader writes about cormorant culling and is most irate that any such thing could occur, and rightly so in my opinion. She says the wildlife in and around Gloucester is generally good, providing excellent nature watching. My columns reach her from a married sister in Cornwall who cuts them out each weekend. Ansome!

*Brimstone Butterfly*

*Red Admiral Butterfly*

*Treecreeper*

Above: *Elf Cup fungi*

Left: *Knapweed*

*Bluebell*

Below left: *Hygrophorus strangulata*

Below right: *Rosehips*

Above: *Seven-spot ladybird on Periwoinkle*

Left: *Trevor on the saltings*

Below: *Willow and Trevor on the saltings*

Another reader phoned re the Zanzibar Red Bishop bird spending time at her South Devon garden, an unusual looking bird and the only Bishop which is black from throat to belly. It is an African species with some kept in captivity in this country so almost certainly it was an escape methinks.

Brian French of Exeter tells me his granddad who lived in Dorset left a diary and in June 1902 saw thousands of terns at Chesil Bank where they bred. What a sight that must have been especially when, he says, they occasionally rose as one, to drop down again for no obvious reason. Brian has kindly sent me the diary to read and it is filled with these wildlife titbits. It is a common occurrence with gulls on mudflats and hereabouts we call these spasmodic movements 'dreads'. Usually there is no reason that we can easily observe and rarely a predator about.

It is of course my duty as a nature writer with, hopefully, readers in the plural, to bring you news of all things bright and beautiful in the natural world. I also keep readers informed and up to date on wildlife matters of all kinds, the good news, the bad and the in between. In fact I reckon the information in this column is as good as it gets anywhere in Britain. Just recently in this very newspaper I have been seeing stuff I mentioned 10 years ago and more but as they say, what goes around comes around. Not only that, new readers emerge who need to be kept up to date, well, not so much up to date, but reminded of things as if they were new.

Shortly a lot of money will be spent on a tawny owl survey. Some say the species is lower in numbers than a few years ago so a costly survey is needed. To help the tawny owl recover its numbers presumably. Well folks all life, especially successful life, relies on habitat that is healthy for each species, with healthy meaning non-polluted, plenty of food etc. etc.

The tawny owl is basically a woodland bird with dispersal needs for its young, some peace and quiet and food, the latter being small mammals in the main. Remove any one of those needs and the result will be less tawny owls. Meddle with all of them, as we are doing, and downhill goes the tawny owl population.

In my neck of the woods tawny owls continue to do very well and from what readers tell me the catchment area of the WMN is good tawny owl country. Better to spend money to buy woodland and look after the wildlife that way. There are woods and land for sale.

On a winter's day when a freezing night has patterned the landscape with white it is a time to pause awhile and drink in the beauty. Then the calls of curlew as several fly overhead. Looking up, there too are many fieldfares and about 50 Canada Geese, unusually silent as they head east upriver.

But for me the unforgettable moment was the frosted buttercup in its tiny little hollow, still in bloom from November and looking as if it is going to remain upright and gold forever. White edged and standing alone in the frost riven grassland there was something symbolic about it, hope I think, and at such moments one feels like sitting in the grass and staying with it. I did crouch by it for a while as Willow searched about, until a female stonechat popped up from a bramble area and then her mate. They nested there last summer so it is their spot, the lone buttercup not so lonely after all.

More geese fly over, silent as the earlier skein, perhaps awed by the frost locked landscape. A black balaclava on top of a great coat said, "nippy isn't it," and the apparition went on by unrecognisable, anonymous.

Out on the mudflats a cormorant runs after a great black-backed gull who has taken its flounder. It is a big fish so the gull can't fly with it. The cormorant enters into a tug of war, both birds flapping their wings and the fish is pulled in half. They both have a meal. Maybe they should work together for they both exploit situations. That is the beginning of co-operation so will we see them 'hand in hand' so to speak? Uneasy partners of need? Dearie me, just like human beings.

It was milder than expected but cloud cover brought its blanket of relative warmth, and rain pattered loud on my shoulders. On a patch of waste ground was an old acacia tree, no doubt correctly known as false acacia and a thorny sort of tree. Just along from it are alder trees, a mix of wild native species and this lone North American introduction. No wonder a few waders from the same country of origin had been about just yards away, paying homage to a 'home' tree species.

Actually 'waste ground' is an unfair name for the spot. It is actually unused by humans, true, but a pretty spot and all the better for wildlife left as it is.

The acacia was planted for timber, used for tool handles and when I checked it out in the books I found it was highly praised in the early 19th century by William Cobbett no less, he of the Rural Rides. So that's led me to read his book, and on life goes with interesting spin-offs.

Alder is common and does well by water here in the Westcountry. It thrives by being able to extract nitrogen from the atmosphere for there tends to be little nitrogen in soil which is water-logged. Nitrogen in essential for plant growth with most plants obtaining it from the soil. In fact the alder trees put more nitrogen into the soil than they use, so build up fertility in the ground.

By the way I recently mentioned you should always inform a landowner if you are about on private land. I should have made it clearer that one should ask permission first, to go on land without public access, which is what I meant by my somewhat vague comment of November time. My thanks to the reader who pointed this out.

Pipits and goldfinches in two distinct flocks of about 30 birds in each were excitedly poking about in the grass not far from a riverbank. We watched until they flew away then went to see what they might have been eating. Chickweed, lots of it, blooming and in seed wherever we looked, a little white starry plant that often blooms in the depth of winter.

Gosh it felt cold and my back trouble was making me pay for walking the very rough terrain. Then my right leg went numb on me again so a pause in my legging it home was the order of the day. Naturally Willow wanted to get on so he picks these times to give me a heftier nudge than usual. Over I go, Willow's look of surprise quite comical as yet again I get closer to Nature. I say something like "that was funny Willow", but he was strolling over to a pretty spaniel with eye lashes, followed by an immaculate owner.

"Did you fall over Mr.Beer?" The Spaniel owner asked the question. "Or have you found something interesting?"

"Bit of both really. One thing leads to another. I was looking at the chickweed and it is a bit short." Well, you have to be all scientific sometimes folks. So we chatted about eating it as a spring salad, or as a vegetable when boiled. I recalled it was also used against rheumatism in ointment form, the herbalist in me always there.

There is also a water-chickweed found on riverbanks and at the edge of my woods, with fleshy leaves that are hairless. It has drooping white flowers and I walked past it for three years before I realised what it was, when I sat down beside it one afternoon.

Bumped into by a roe deer, and then a pheasant. Life is scary. It was 7am, dark and still, the very high tide showing through the trees, the water lit by orange glints from lights across the river. I unlocked back gate, stepped into the lane with Willow and thump! Into my legs at knee height the shoulders of a roe deer, obviously jumpy at my sudden appearance in the woods, gave me a resounding wallop as off it ran.

That was it. Willow seeing me collecting my thoughts and walking stick from the dark floor, barked in support of my own comments and I felt another thud and a flurry of feathers flapping in my face. 'Kok, kok,kok,' came the familiar sound of a pheasant as I sat on back step deciding whether to venture further or go back indoors and start again.

So Willow had an early breakfast and I made a muggatee. My spectacles had mud all over one lens as did my hair and beard. What a strange world it is. Anyway, cleaned up and ready to go the intrepid nature watcher and his trusty companion set off in the first light, the lane now empty of large, swift moving live missiles. Strewth! Think how frightened they must have been. Blimmin humans, about in the dark woods. Stupid.

Down by the Dripping Well a water rail called to the dawn light. I jumped, expected another 'attack' but all was peaceful. Yes, water rails do call aloud in winter, not only in the breeding season and it is an unearthly sound. That and foxes calling can put your nerves on edge. Too much excitement for one day. Shan't look in a mirror when I get home. That would really be too much.

Two whooper swans watched us as we ambled along the earth bank between the river and a marsh pool. They are big swans, like our resident mute swans, and hold their necks straight, the black and yellow bill helping identification. I doubt they'll stay around. Possibly they will leave and end up at Slimbridge where winter flocks are an annual sight. Years ago we found a pair of whooper swans nesting by a small loch in northern Scotland, adding to a wonderful holiday there.

There is also the winter visiting Bewick Swan which reaches us from Siberia. My first encounter with the species was on the Somerset Levels in the 1950s, the most recent, on the Caen River at Braunton near the moored boats. The Bewick is a smaller white swan than the other two mentioned and has a rounded yellow patch at the base of its bill whereas the Whooper has a distinctly triangular wedge of a patch.

Beautiful here, wild in that wintry way the Westcountry provides us all, perfectly stated by a lone greenshank standing elegantly in the marsh pool, reflected into the darkly green waters.

200 or so wigeon sit out on the water. Attractive ducks wigeon. A friend always spells it Widgeon, which I see some Americans do, but as with pigeon, the letter 'D' was omitted years ago. Apparently the 'D' was dropped as a conservation matter, to save ink. Here in the Westcountry us locals often drop our 'Hs', specially if it's to ev a muggatee but the letter occasionally bounces back in happles and such. Ansome local dialect. Must preserve it. Well folks, I be gwane to take me dugout now, down thicky lane and back afore it tips down, tis black's yer 'at over Bill's mother's agane. Ev a lovely weekend.

A barn owl hunted the frosted field as redwings sought haws in a hedgerow which had an abundance of the red berries a week or so ago. This if the real winter, not so much of the calendar as of the feel, and the shortage of food for some wild creatures which need warming food each day. It was two O'clock in the afternoon and very cold, the owl hunting in daylight to eat to stay alive.

It is as basic as that really. Whilst it is true we, too, eat to live, birds and many other small creatures cannot cope with just a few hours without food in these cold conditions.

Seeing a barn owl in daylight is a treat all the same and I could not bring myself to turn away and miss a while longer in its domain. After flying low over the field for a while it gave a scritch, then perched on the nearest post of a fence line, to stare intently into the grasses. Gradually the owl worked its way along the fence, post hopping, until it suddenly dropped, pounced in something, its wings mantling its prey.

Ah well, it had caught a meal so there was food about for the diligent seeker. How different it is to have a pantry, and shops. The barn owl's fresh, warm food would stay it for a while.

The mantling, holding the wings partly open, is the owl's way of hiding its prey from the eyes of others. In the heron it is a method of seeing more clearly down into water, especially on very bright days, the bird more easily able to catch a fish. Try it if you are gazing into a pool, to see things better I mean, not to catch fish.

A most peculiar thing and one I haven't seen before. I had followed Willow down a lane to a stream and fields. The waterway was in spate and where I used to cross was impossible so I detoured to find a little bridge. Even here the water was up to the planks and all was very slippery so I decided to remain where I was as my back and right leg were in enough trouble. Willow didn't mind, he is one for nosing around inquisitively.

And there by the stone wall dividing two fields was a group of roe deer, such a group or herd as I have not seen together. Thirty roe deer! Perhaps some readers see this many gathered at one time but it is well beyond the rut and there were bucks, does and kids in their first year in the group, a real winter herd. Two bucks began to stamp their feet, looking across the water at us then in a neat bunch they walked quite casually away into the woods a field away. There was no panic and I was rather disappointed to have favoured binocular over camera but there tis.

A look around showed good grass all along the wall line so I think the deer had chosen to graze together and shelter this side of the wall. It was mild and still but the previous night had been very windy onto the other side of the wall where a drift of leaves lay along its length. Roe are predominantly browsers but they do occasionally graze. They are dusk to dawn feeders in the main.

So a fascinating morning. Must go back and do a bit of scouting about to see if the roe remain in the area, as a herd or whether they soon disperse.

Walking through some 'scrub' the word flashed through my mind, as to what scrub is. Usually it is 'unfarmable' land or woodland that has been cleared and allowed to do its own thing, with shrubs and a natural regeneration of trees coming back. Often the term 'scrub' is used in a derogatory way by 'authorities' wanting to support development proposals. In fact, where scrub survives it is excellent for wildlife, providing nest sites for birds, shelter, food and cover for many species and it usually has an interesting flora. A bit more praise for scrub with promotion for it as an important habitat type would be nice to see.

The patch we were in has two orchid species, saplings, meadowsweet and yellow flag, several bird species including breeding birds, ferns, bramble and a number of small mammals. It is good for snails, has many insects and a host of wildflowers. It is also a perfect 'classroom' for observing Nature's changes over the years, all the more beautiful for being left to its own devices.

Badger and fox went along a muddy track. A mistle thrush sang as it swayed at the top of a birch sapling. It was lovely to hear it do so in winter accompanied by the fluting song of a robin, as a couple of wrens flitted about in dense herbage. Bird song it is rightly called I suppose but one cannot help thinking of various birds each having their own musical instruments at times, their own pastoral symphony.

On the ground a broken white egg shell. Above, the rough stick platform nest of a wood pigeon tells the story of early nesting and probable hatching of one or two young. Well that's my first nest for 2005, it is usually a pigeon or a blackbird that sets the ball rolling.

Catkins everywhere from around 5th January developed quickly into a delightful highway and byway sight. Along with the real lamb's tails bobbing about in fields as the little sheep gambolled in the wind and rain one felt the 'pull' of springtime's magic.

Hazel and birch are probably our best known catkin bearers and in birches male catkins are formed in the autumn to mature in March and April when they hang freely from the ends of twigs. Hazel catkins expand in the first mild weather of the new year. If the air is calm little pollen escapes from the catkin but a good blow sends clouds of pollen about.

All of us must surely have certain sights, sounds and smells which trigger our zestfulness, whatever time of year it is and I feel it is good to recall those to mind and maybe deliberately set out to enjoy and sense them if one feels a bit 'flat'. It is easy for me as the countryside and natural history is the mainstream of my life so I'm tuned in to Mother Nature's delights.

But if you are feeling a bit under the weather nature's tonics are always there to lift us and I must say, seeing the first lesser celandines on January 11th really did make my day despite the huge gales and heavy rain of that time.

But back to catkin bearing trees a favourite of mine is the alder, companion tree to waterways and wet places, the sort of haunts I love to spend time in. To see the alder bearing the long male and much shorter female catkins or inflorescences in early Spring is a joy. Immediately I seek out primroses and then listen each day for the first chiff chaff song. Now that's ansome!

Ground ivy in flower, pretty early I reckon, and thriving here in the woods and along the hedgebank. It does not look like ivy nor is it related to it so a misleading English name really. It is an attractive plant and its other name Alehoof reminds us it is a herb once used in brewing to clear beer and give it a better flavour. I'd better way have a ground ivy sandwich occasionally methinks.

Gill tea is made from the plant, a strengthening and cleansing tonic of a drink. Monkey Chops, Blue Runner and Rabbit's Mouth's are country names which aptly describe the flower, the leaves of which were used to stuff meat dishes, particularly roast pork. Tunfoot is another old name telling of its use in brewing ale, then along came hops and ground ivy enjoys a quieter life in the wilds and some gardens.

Watching a great spotted woodpecker, a male with a red nape, tapping away at the top of an oak branch I was close enough to see that every time a gull or other bird flew over the trees, it ducked then resumed its search for insects. Ducking, an age old safety device we all use instinctively and here the woodpecker was quite exposed on a branch top. It wasn't that any of the birds flying over was a predator but here was a bird busily feeding, with that natural awareness there just may be a sparrowhawk about. Flattening to the branch may cause a predator to miss, or help the woodpecker appear part of the branch it was perched upon. Most birds are both predator and prey species, the woodpecker requiring large numbers of insects and other live food in order to survive, as do so many others of our avian friends.

A foxes scream rents the air, an almost full moon lending an eerie atmosphere to a night when our exhaled breaths hung on the air. Willow was a white furry low cloud up ahead, enjoying his regular night walk before turning in til the morrow. Slim white shapes in a row where the underwood joins the field were night roosting egrets dreaming of fish filled rivers. They can be seen most nights when the south westerly prevailing winds blow over the tree tops and miss them. Come the dawn a few wing flaps carries them to the creeks, pools and river where they can dab for an early breakfast.

Dab is also a name given to several right- sided flatfish some of which frequent the Westcountry's sandy bars, just as are flounders and the witches of deeper waters.

The lone Bewick swan could just be seen, straight necked, on the grass by the water's edge. It has been around a while which messes up my predication the bird would not stay more than a day or two. It is watching the water in the relative darkness instead of taking a nap with head tucked beneath one wing. Perhaps the fox we heard is way out on the saltings seeking supper.

Dark shapes like grass tussocks show as we reach our turning point. The moon lights them but sits them in their own dark shadows. Dark in dark, Canada geese, silent. If one sees us there'll be a right old song and dance. We turn away sharply and Willow speeds up. He favours the homeward direction in this cold for there is always a wind at night its seems. The night's chill breath which is sometimes stilled by the dawn. Bedtime Willow, I say.

Soil creep in the steep woods, that gradual downhill movement caused by summer heat and rain taking loose soil particles to lower areas. Where we stand it has formed a rather nice row taken over by primroses and violets. Now more soil creep is building up material for a wildflower spread and it is interesting to note the very attractive changes. It is a reminder, also, that no matter how aware we are of a particular area, even if it always seems to look the same it actually never is.

Change is often so subtle. For example a favourite spot, at the edge of one wood I frequent, has had sweet woodruff growing for as long as I can remember. The old fence looks the same and I can virtually guarantee blackcaps will nest just up from the woodruff as the little warbler species has done for 40 years. Obviously they can't be the ones I nest monitored originally but the little dell twixt woods and rough grassland field is real blackcap country. Joy of a place to sit on a summer day, here one can relax and listen to the songs of birds and bees and watch the blackcaps about their business.

Perhaps the bramble there has increased slightly, the trees have thickened and the gorse by the sheep tracks running horizontally along the hill slope is more straggly, but little else has altered. This was 'my' spot when I was a slip of a lad learning about birds and animals. Flowers came later. The person may age but the magic remains. Getting hooked on nature watching at an early age is a most beautiful thing. It is never too late of course, the most fascinating pastime of all.

John Buchan it was who said that one of the greatest misfortunes of advancing age is that you get out of touch with the sunrise. Personally I don't find that. Not yet anyway and I see a whole lot of dawns, thanks greatly to Willow. I'm an out and about person anyway, especially in the early hours when one rarely sees anyone else about. I also enjoy a late night look along the lane so maybe I was an owl in another life, or am building up to becoming one. But dogs get you out and on the move, keeping ones joints from rusting.

Lots of celandines about in woods and hedges now, a lovely spring flower. I should say lesser celandine, for there is also the greater though they are unrelated. They are both celandines because both used to bloom in ancient Greece at the time when swallows, chelidon in Greek, arrived.

Here we tend to go more in for 'cuckoo' names to signify Spring plants but we do have Swallow-grundy and Swallow Wort.

Swallow Grundy is one of the local names given to groundsel, also known as Canary Food, Groundwill, and Yellowheads. However 'swallow' is nothing to do with the bird but refers to the plant swallowing the ground if it is left unattended when crops have been harvested, particularly early potatoes. Groundsel was once a popular medicinal herb so the birds that love it know what they are about.

Swallow Wort is the Greater Celandine, also known as Kill-Wart, wart plant, witches Flower and Yellow Spit. Break the stem and a drop of orange liquid comes out, the 'yellow spit' to apply to warts and cure them. The juice was also used to cure eye problems. Herbal cures and teas, wonderful.

15 pheasant eggs, beautiful olive green, lay where a hen pheasant had just departed so we had to quickly and obviously move away to let her know all was well. It is a fairly early nest and with eggs laid at 24 hour intervals she had been working hard. However, the eggs all hatch together because incubation does not begin until the last egg is laid.

Chicks are born downy and capable of feeding themselves from birth. For the first few days they usually rely for food on the store of yolk carried in their bellies.

We went off to a safe distance and watched the female move through the undergrowth to return to her eggs within 90 seconds which I felt showed her keenness and our common sense to have cleared off. I feel 15 eggs is about a maximum clutch size for one female and she will take between 23 and 28 days to hatch them.

I have just got some good photos of a jay which flew down to the woodland floor to begin picking over leaf litter, presumably to find cached acorns. I'd actually gone out to take pot luck on a sunny day and was about to photograph wild arum leaves backlit by the sun when the jay suddenly appeared. The choice was obvious, the wild arum or parson in the pulpit will be around for weeks, a jay close by on the ground might not.

Large holes in oak marble galls showed where birds had been at them, possibly the greater spotted woodpecker we now see most days. I've got some good shots of that too, so am well pleased with winter photography. In woodlands, with the leaves off the trees the light is often brighter and thus the conditions for photography are better.

I wish colours had been given natural names when it came to naming paints. I know a few have but to have agaric red or beech bark grey would be rather useful. It is just the idea of the colour, the eye-sense of it that would appeal but then there are so many shades and tones in nature, I suppose we can make up the colours we need. I love mucking about in paints as much as old Ratty loved mucking about in boats.

Actually I'm a sepia and Payne's grey fan who likes a splash of bright colour here and there when the mood takes me. Yesterday a treecreeper on an oak tree trunk was stunning, and then the first coltsfoot flowers on February 13th were magical in driving hail. I just stood and stared with stinging ears as jackdaws fought to stay on course in the gale, making sure but difficult headway til they dropped, thankfully I felt sure, into the trees.

The mewing of a cat came loud. Willow pointed to where a bedraggled black cat with white paws lay beneath a fallen branch. I hauled the timber away, picking the sodden creature up, drying it best I could with my handkerchief. Yellow eyes glittered at me and the cat began to purr, a good sign. Willow trotted off ahead and I followed, decided to take the cat home as I thought I knew where it lived. Sure enough, about 50 paces from our gate, a huge wriggle and out of my arms it leapt to race along the lane and in via its own back gate.

A lucky cat and seemingly unharmed, going by its speedy gallop homeward. Nine lives, very useful with branches falling about in storms. We've seen it about since then, a bit of a prowler but handsome with it.

Rustic humour has about it something that is lacking elsewhere and these days there is a lot of elsewhere. I heard that a fellow buying a horse from another, asked if it kicked. The owner said, 'not what you call kick exactly, but she'll lift a hind leg sudden and bring it back smartish. Best to step out of the way when she does that!'

I shall include a bit of humour more often in this column, specially if it's a maze Monday like today. We need to laugh and I can't keep on looking in the mirror.

The term 'alien' crops up regularly these days re animals and plants. I was reading an old report on sheep wool from the 1960s and was surprised to find that Wool Aliens were once carefully recorded. These are plants whose seeds have become tangled in sheep's wool in Australia and other countries which exported wool to us. These germinated and grew in our fields where wool waste, or shoddy, was commonly used as manure. A list of 530 species, including 187 grasses was compiled in 1961.

I'm sure many readers have observed the usual plants popping up in soil beneath bird tables, from the various bird foods we put out for our feathered friends. Our own diet has altered tremendously in recent years with the huge amounts of foreign foods on sale, and now our birds and other wildlife species are having to similarly adapt.

We do our utmost to buy local and eat and drink 'organic' so most of the 'orts' I put out for the birds is homely fare. There is usually a queue waiting in the mornings so I hope we are doing right.

Windflower in bloom, the lovely wood anemone, often abundant in Westcountry woodlands. Where I live it carpets the wood floor, a joy to see along with lesser celandines. My mother called wood anemone granny's nightcap, a well known local name for this plant with its feathery leaves. Even when the flowers are up and over the leaves will be found to midsummer, building food reserves for the next year.

Any moment now the few hibernators will emerge, hedgehogs, dormice and such, from their winter sojourn. The cold end to February, into March, was like the old days when winter was winter. Those few mild winters in succession helped quite a few species to pick up their numbers and I rarely have a day go by without seeing a kingfisher.

Yesterday in deep woods we heard the 'whoo' song of a long eared owl very clearly. It is low, rather melancholy in tone and off repeated. It is a species more common than some say, but overlooked due to its reclusive ways and secluded habitats. Here in the Westcountry it is a wintering bird from colder climes and also a breeding species albeit not in large numbers.

A reader phoned re a whitethroat singing in a Cornish country churchyard on February 20th. That, I would say, was a whitethroat that stayed on, over-wintered with us rather than an early incoming migrant from Africa. Blackcaps and chiff chaffs tend to be the commonest 'stayers', both visiting our gardens regularly. I have a very nice 35mm colour transparency of a chiff chaff in the snow and now here they are, coming back to gladden the spring and summer for us. Another phone call, 'an osprey in a tree by the Tamar estuary', this on the 22nd February, so a few about.

It was very interesting last week to visit a coastal area with several caves, to find five of the numerous pigeons living there had rings on their legs. No rock doves of course, all the other pigeons, feral and in all probability the ex racing pigeons were breeding with these. Well, life is sweet here on what are sunny south facing cliffs with ample food and shelter so the pigeons had chosen a life by the seaside and seemed in fine fettle. All five ringed birds were on site a week later and we saw two more in a similar situation about half a mile away.

Grey seals still breed occasionally in our caves, One I know which slopes up to a high rocky shelf with sand being popular with this mammal. The sand ledge is out of reach of high tides so ideal for any pups born.

Caves are odd places, almost entirely devoid of plant life within yet the entrance may well support high levels of seaweed just as on the rocky shore. Quite frequently a ledge over the outside of a cave may have luxuriant displays of pink thrift and other plants whilst rabbits crop the cliff top above.

Light plays an important part in seaweed growth with the red seaweeds better able to survive in darker cave interior situations. They can more easily absorb the blue-green light needed for photosynthesis than the brown and green seaweeds.

Sea caves often appear where the pounding of the sea wears away the rock at a weak point in the cliff face. Blow holes may appear where the cliff top subsides and at promontories continuing erosion often creates an arch. Stacks are created when the roof of an arch collapses, and so on.

The spread of plant life is intriguing, some species increasing their range into unexpected territory, true migration often defying book information. A plant I'm very fond of for its prettiness and splashes of summer whiteness is scurvy grass, of the Cochlearia family though perhaps I should say 'grasses' as both Common and English may be found. They are tiny members of the cabbage family and books quite rightly give their natural habitat as muddy places around the coast and on saltmarshes.

However, scurvy grass is rapidly spreading inland and found mainly along hedgerows by roadsides yet often not in hedgerows nearby but away from roads. I found this puzzling as it is much the same as Alexanders, another plant found more commonly inland these days yet once thought of as 'coastal' to about 4-6 miles inland.

Coastal. The common factor with so many plants of the coast is tolerance to salt. But let's take that more sensibly forward. A liking for salt, plants that have evolved with adaptations for surviving in salty conditions eventually need those conditions as being right for them, necessary then.

We have been constantly putting down salt on many roads to combat icy conditions, much of it spraying into hedge banks as vehicles drive through it. A highways worker confirmed that roads I mentioned where scurvy grass is now common over 20 miles from the coast, were salt treated. This gradual build up of salt has created a 'coastal' mud type habitat inland, possibly to the detriment of some plants which do not like salt but a gain for scurvy grass. One wonders how the various animals associated with these old hedgerows are faring now they have salt with their greens. As far as I know this situation has not yet been studied.

We were exploring a secluded North Devon cove with a very pretty beach, high cliffs and a rocky shore. Though it was 3pm in the afternoon there wasn't a footprint anywhere, no Man Friday or any of that stuff. A pair of wheatears were flitting about after insects, the first together pair I'd seen for the year. They certainly don't hang about once they arrive here.

Anyway, I took a closer look at some of the insects about in the sunshine around the edges of rock crevices. This is when using ones binocular reversed as a sort of microscope come in very handy. I also use one of those tubes about the size of a camera film container, with a magnifying lens at one end. They, too, are excellent in the field.

And so we found lots of the Marine Bug (*Aepophilus bonnairei*) a creature that hides in rock crevices and hunts only when the rocks are above water. I did not know its scientific name of course, had to seek it out in books. It seems that breeding is more or less continuous, with adults and young found all the year round. The Marine Bug is quite a local species so once again North Devon turns up trumps, a remarkable area for wildlife even in these sorry times of declines.

These tiny bugs are predators themselves, yet fall foul of larger predators, including the wheatears and other birds which haunt these delightful coastal habitats. No-one much comes to this spot, the local and tourism honey spot areas about half a mile away so the wildlife gains hugely from the seclusion. Perhaps that is why this little bug is successful here, relict from the days when Brittany was reachable on foot from our own mainland.

The great spotted woodpecker has been drumming away since the week before Easter and I see he has a mate. Quite a few people along the lane have remarked on the far carrying sound. We are fortunate as it is right behind our property so I can stand and watch this remarkable bird behaviour from back gate.

I've been compiling a countryside encyclopaedia, or sort of A-Z for several months, my latest entry being zygodactyle. It is a word coined for birds with two toes pointing forwards and two backwards, as in the woodpeckers. So there you go, the Zs completed. ZZZ; time to rest and doze in a garden chair. I began the pleasant task with Aaron's Rod, a name given to the common mullien plant. Ansome!

Had a lovely letter from an 8 year old girl reader who lives some three miles from here, and a 12 year old boy from Exeter, the same day. Just coincidence but both sent lists of what they see in their home patch and both enjoy their binoculars so much. I feel it is one way to get youngsters interested in nature, the binocular. The difference in bringing a scene of a bird or other animal close to, so that every detail and movement is visible never ceases to be magical.

The girl says her favourite at present is a pair of moorhens nesting just 100 metres from where she lives. She can watch them through some trees and she wants to be an artist when she grows up. Well let's wish her well. Obviously youngsters do enjoy newspapers, or bits in them and I felt quite lifted to hear from that pre-teen age group, and have enjoyed writing back to them. I did so love the years I ran a Field Club for youngsters. Good days.

There's no doubt about it, just at the moment, with the breeding season for birds barely underway the countryside is teeming with life. Certainly in my neck of the woods all looks very well with the possibility of a bumper year in prospect. In fact it is so active in the woods, fields and lanes I spend much of my time in that I hardly known where to look first. All I can suggest is that a lot of birds and other animals had a very good winter. I have even found a 'new' water vole site, new to me at any rate but no doubt the voles have known about it for years. It is by a waterway on a busy farm, the water voles above a weir. Seeing two on a spring day, fresh after a night of rain was special indeed.

Later in the year we can usually attribute increased bird activity to successful breeding with many young of the year about, but not as yet so the signs are good thus far.

Our local tawny owls have two young already. I was watching and listening to the great spotted woodpecker calling 'tjick-tjick', when I saw two downy owls eyeing me solemnly from an oak branch. The tree is on such a steep slope that from my vantage point above it the owls appeared only 6ft from the ground but in fact they were some 20ft up. Somewhere nearby the adult tawnies would be watching, ready to defend their young if necessary. I do hope we don't have any moaning stories this year from people warned off a nesting area by owls or whatever. If you get a clip round the ear from some winged creature then move out of its domain is the thing to do.

Lady walking home along the river bank, from the market, stopped to chat about the lack of birds on the river so I explained most have gone off to their breeding haunts. Then she said she had just bought a swede to cook with a meal and on the way home she'd wondered why they are called Swedes.

The root crop was once known as Swedish turnips, simply because they were introduced from Sweden. The swede has a greater food value for humans and animals than turnips and is closer textured. Swedes do very well in cool areas, with large crops grown. On a farm across the river from our place I recall fields where they grew and sheep would be put out to forage on them. I believe movable fences were used to ensure systematic feeding, possibly electric fences though I've no idea when they were introduced.

"Well that has sorted out Swedes for me," she said when I'd explained, "so you can now tell me this. Along the path to the old Well there is a hawthorn still with all its berries, yet the others have more or less been stripped. Why is that?"

Trouble is I don't know the answer. I know the tree well and pass it two or three times a day. It is a lone hawthorn in that it grows across the path from the others which form a long hedge. However, it's only a stride away and is still full of haws. Shortly they will be pushed of by this year's growth but they would have made a few good meals for hungry birds.

I said I was as flummoxed as she and I'd throw out a query on it to readers. It is a healthy hawthorn which leafs and blossoms well like those nearby.

If you want to see pied flycatchers this summer then do try the walk from the Horner Valley and Stoke Pero on Exmoor. A reader phoned to ask where she and her family could see this lovely summer visiting bird and the walk is one of the finest, sheltered walks through a wooded valley. Visit, too, Stoke Pero's isolated church. And if you cant get to Exmoor, try Dartmoor's lovely Yarner Wood for the species.

Stoke Pero church is the highest on Exmoor at over 1000ft (300m). The timbers for the new roof (1897) were pulled up from Porlock by a donkey named Zulu whose photo is in the church. What a task!

I am fortunate enough to have 6-8 pairs of pied flycatchers at the Sanctuary, all in nestboxes. That is good along with other species, the woods very attractive and excellent wildlife habitat.

Pied flycatcher males are black and white, the females brown and white. 6-7, usually 7 bright blue eggs are laid in May and incubated by the female for 13-14 days, during which time she is fed by the male. Both adults feed the young which fledge at around 14 days. Food is mainly insects caught on the wing, or on the ground, they also take insect larvae, mites and other invertebrates.

As with spotted flycatchers usually only one brood a year is raised. I've personally never known two broods. Pied flycatchers take readily to hole type nest boxes whereas spotted flycatchers prefer the open fronted ones. Both species may be found in the same broadleaved woodland, the pied arriving before the spotted, I find.

Westcountry moors are delightful at this time of year and have some really good way- marked path routes.

We were well up along a favourite waterway on a pleasant spring day, the weekend bringing out quite a few walkers. Two youngsters on the bank had small nets and jam jars, which took me back a few years. We ambled over, Willow taking advantage of a drink where water rushed sparkling over rocks.

"Do you know what fish this is Mr. Beer? My brother's just caught it," asked the girl of the two.

The fish was a stone loach, the commonest of our two loaches and one I often caught here as a lad, along with minnows and sticklebacks. I told them about the stone loach and its secretive ways in daylight and they agreed they'd just been poking nets in the dense weed and hoping.

I told them the loach will now be into spring spawning from April to May, with eggs shed amongst the water plants or on gravel. In a couple of weeks the eggs hatch and after a few days the young fry begin feeding on algal detritus. Stone loaches become mature at 2 years and live to about 7 years maximum.

"So we ought to put it back then, not take it home? They looked a bit disappointed but cheered up when I said creatures living in moving water may die in still water and keeping them in a jar would be bad really. I said to have a close look, perhaps do a few sketches and then release them quickly is better. I gave them a note of two or three books that would help identify waterway life, and my note pad and pencil.

Within a minute or two the girl had drawn a very good stone loach, then began to sketch the primroses. Back to its home went the loach and we left two happy youngsters on the riverbank.

ᴥ❀ᴥ

A reader writes having enjoyed the amusing story of the fellows discussing whether a horse kicked or not. So, yer be a couple more m'dears. What about the farm labourer deploring a townies ignorance. "Ee knows no more about farmin' than a cow does about Sundays."

And the countryman who said to his neighbour when they met in town, "Are you out for a days enjoyment, or is your wife with ee?"

Dearie me, now I'll be in trouble. But I love chatting to country folk. Just last week I was telling an elderly chappie how our cowslips had flowered on April 1st and he said, better if you grow cabbages. He had his mind set on cabbages that suit small spaces and told me a garden without a cabbage is like a house without a door. I didn't realise there was a cabbage called the Paignton. Ned used to grow them and said they came late but grew huge, good quality, and very sweet, he said.

As it is I've often planted cabbages and lettuces up along the edge of flower and shrub borders. Many are very attractive and it's good to cut fresh vegetables. For the 10 years we had Grey, our squirrel, we grew lots of cherry tomatoes as he loved his tasty treats and was a real gentleman, loving and well mannered.

Mike, along the lane, put in his seed spuds on Good Friday. He chuckles at my folklore beliefs but I notice he follows some of them and touches his hat to magpies. Ned also grew up with the old ways, his garden lovely, brimming with flowers but it has to feed him and wife as well. That's the point of having a plot of ground he reckons. Can't argue with that.

Watching the stoat lope off amongst the mist of bluebells (yesterday's W.M.N) I got down on my hands and knees to examine the chewed bluebell, then took a squizz along its route. It pays sometimes when studying wildlife to get down to the level of other creatures to better understand their world. Then one knows why the sense of smell is so important to many a hunter. They simply cannot see very far even with good eyesight. Try it. Even getting down to the head height of a fox, or your dog or cat, and world becomes a very different place.

The stoat had run off along a narrow but distinct path. Possibly it is one of its regular runs from which to pick up on scents. Once 'fixed' upon a quarry stoats, and weasels too, follow up on their prey in relentless fashion. I've seen stoats hunt down a rabbit and follow it straight through a whole group of rabbits, unwavering, whilst they watched, knowing they were safe until the next time so to speak. I've also seen the occasional buck rabbit, master of his warren, kick a stoat flying with his hind legs. The life of the predator isn't always one way. Maybe eating bluebells is safer.

Two nuthatches have taken one of our nest boxes. Well, it is still on its tree, 'taken' it as a home for nesting and raising a brood of young. We watch them wing flicking in display then off they go chasing happily amongst the trees. For a few days we will hear them in noisy display, days of calls and song then once they get down to breeding and eggs are laid they'll go quiet, so quiet one might think they have gone elsewhere. Must get my hide erected.

Superb male pheasant in the garden, bronze and scarlet in bright sunshine. I took a couple of photographs, then it walked sedately off to doze in the sun out of the cold north wind. What a privilege for us that was, aided by the fact we live adjoining woodland. Speckled wood butterflies spiralling about and quite a few green shield bugs on buddleia and hawthorn, the latter common in the Westcountry in many a garden.

The coarse grasses of the woods and lanes suit the speckled wood as foodplants. Eggs are laid singly on grass blades. These early speckled woods emerge in April and May from the chrysalis. This is the only British butterfly that hibernates either as larva or a pupa, almost as if according to choice. A good species to study as it is about for the entire spring and summer, often well into the autumn.

Wait for the insect to perch. The wings of the female are more rounded, but look also for the broad patch of darker, velvety scent scales across the forewings of males. I find some of the old books are better identification guides than modern ones but they can be hefty and no use in the field. 'Collins Field Guide to the Butterflies of Britain & Europe' by Tom Tolman is very good and available in shops. There is also one on caterpillars, by Carter & Hargreaves. Good hunting.

As I write this there is a garden warbler in the garden. It has only just arrived so I shall try to get photos. The quietly coloured bird tends to hide so it wont be easy. If anything its best field character is its lack of distinguishing marks, yet tis a pretty bird with a pleasant song similar to that of the closely related blackcap.

I like to think that the notable increase of brimstone butterflies at one or two woodland sites near my home is partly due to the many alder buckthorn trees we've planted. All are doing well. It has an odd English name for it has no thorns and is not related to the alder tree as was once thought. The flowers are tiny, greenish yellow and borne singly or in clusters in the angle between the leaf stalks and the stems. Both male and female parts are borne in the same flower. Inconspicuous they may be to us but they attract many bees, wasps and flies by the well exposed nectar. These do the vital job of pollination when they brush the five short, purple stamens that are closely bent in towards the stigma.

Green berries follow the flowers, these turning red by July, and velvet black by the end of August. These ripen and fall from September to November depending when in the summer the flowers appeared. Birds and small mammals eat the berries. Our wood mice carry them off to make neat little piles with them or store them in disused bird's nests, whilst thrushes such as redwings and fieldfares may carry them long distances, shedding them in their droppings.

My main objective in planting 150 alder buckthorn trees was to help the brimstone butterfly but it is good to see the spin-off gains and the beauty of the plant itself. It is an interesting little tree, a shrub in some habitats, that does not harmfully compete with other tree species and does a lot of good.

Along with purging buckthorn, alder buckthorn is a vital foodplant for brimstone butterflies which lay in May to produce a July generation that hibernates as adults, often hidden in ivy covered trees.

Orange tip butterflies about since 13th April, always a lovely sight. They coincided with the first flowering of Jack-by-the-hedge, one of my favourite wild flowers, and an orange tip food plant along with milkmaids, the lovely Lady's Smock or cuckoo flower.

Robin saw house martins flying up river on 8th April, over the Taw River, and numerous 7 spot ladybirds, scores of them, so I would not wish to be an aphid this year. By the time you read this most if not all our incoming migrant birds will be in and nesting, a wonderful time of year.

This afternoon I thought our forsythia flowers were taking off to fly around my head when a male blackbird alighted momentarily. He was chasing off three others and what a kerfuffle there was. But the flying yellows were three Speckled Yellow Moths, on the wing rather early I thought, but such pretty insects. It is a day flying species which uses wood sage, woundworts and deadnettles as larval food plants, so is a woodland wanderer. Look for a warmly toned yellow moth with striking dark markings on the wings. The caterpillar is green.

The moth has an incredible scientific name *Pseudopanthera macularia*. Pseudos for false, and panthera from the dark spots on a yellow ground cover. Macularia, from macula, a spot, the 'speckled yellow'. Once you start to tackle scientific names via their meanings it all begins to make sense. So they tell me.

Hoof marks in the lane today, the rain making life interesting. Roe Deer by the look of them, an animal which hides by day and comes out to feed around dusk and dawn time. Other tracks included moorhen, heron, badger and squirrel, history in the mud! Ansome!

A reader writes to ask 'what is a sea hare?' It is a smallish 3-6ins olive-green to red brown animal which somewhat resembles a crouching hare. Its scientific name is *Aplysia punctata* and it lives offshore amongst seaweed. It moves about on a single foot like snails do but occasionally swims by flapping the lobes of its foot. It has tentacles which resemble hares ears.

Sea hares feed on common sea lettuce. If disturbed they may release a purple slime which stains, though it is not a fast dye like the sepia from cuttle fish. They cross fertilise one another as do snails and often mate in chains. During the summer they move up to the inter-tidal zone to spawn and lay strings of eggs on rocks or weeds, after which they die. These eggs hatch into larvae which eventually became adults.

Lovely time of year, now, to wander Westcountry beaches to see what's about. Do remember to be sure of tide times and if amongst sand dunes, keep to well worn paths as these habitats are fragile and vulnerable as is the wildlife associated with them. And if you are on the coast path take care, you may find you are quite fragile yourself if you fall. I am constantly surprised to see walkers in such places wearing slippery soled 'town' shoes. And with the warmer weather on the way avoid dehydration. I know a fit fellow who collapsed on a walk around the Cornish Coast and it was all about not taking in water en route. Get a goodly sized hip flask from an Army Surplus Store, and what about a nice chunk of Kendal Mint Cake, the National Trust shops usually stock it.

Had not seen a lesser spotted woodpecker for a while then suddenly there one was, a smart little male with a red crown. He was low down in a thicket of ash and wild cherry at one end of a large oak wood, well, mainly oak and there were we sitting on bin liners munching sandwiches. Such small woodpeckers, about sparrow size and with that lovely black and white barring across the back that is so characteristic of the species. Females have black crowns, and there is no red on the under tail coverts as there is in the greater spotted woodpecker.

Listen for the piercing 'kee-kee-kee'. Both the male and female drum, somewhat more weakly than the great spotted yet with long lasting and high pitched sequences of blows.

Oak, sycamore, alder and various fruit trees such as the wild cherry may be chosen for nesting holes and they may be low down (18ins) above the ground or way up around 21ft (7m) high. They are cosy nest sites lined with rotting wood, the eggs laid in May or June usually. Incubation is around 2 weeks, but both male and female, the young becoming fully fledged at about 21 days. Only one brood each year is raised.

This woodpecker feeds almost exclusively on insects, in summer aphids, ants and beetles, as well as various flies, small butterflies and their larvae. In winter they seek insect pupae as a main source of food and may visit more rural or secluded bird tables.

Time permitting I shall discover the nest site ere long and perhaps obtain a photograph of this elusive little bird but for now, just seeing it is exciting and is what nature watching is all about. Knowing the little fellow is here, alive and well feels good.

Swifts over the marshes, flying low to hawk insects on a grey day, one of the countless superb sights of a Westcountry morning. Their screaming 'scree-scree'scree' calls sound loud as they fly low overhead at speeds that has a body wondering how they catch their prey. These days the swift nests mostly with us in our various buildings but once upon a time they would have nested in caves and cliff crevices, perhaps also in hollow trees and such.

This week we saw swifts entering an old church tower as we looked around a churchyard. The birds often nest in caves in cliffs and elsewhere where natural shelters gave them dwelling places. Now they live with us in a variety of our hand built sites, even in towns and the edges of cities. Look for them clinging to the stonework of buildings before entering whatever hole leads in to eggs or young, not the commonest sight for most of a swift's life is spent on the wing. What an incredible life!

I see cuckoo spit has been about since May Day on a variety of plants, so the young froghoppers have been blowing bubbles to protect themselves, probably from predators and sunshine too. It is a phenomenon we shall see all summer in our gardens as well as in the wild.

Found a 'new' plant in the woods behind our home, growing by a spring in a pleasant dell. It is thyme leaved speedwell, one of those pretty blue forget-me-not type flowers and a good find. That is four different speedwells we have found in these woods now including common germander speedwell. Always pays to take a closer look at the flora and fauna.

About 100 yards of razor shells, lots of them, along a quiet, secluded beach reachable by a precarious path which I remember as being much safer than it is today. Lack of use by locals who used to fish from the rocks and enjoy the sunshine days with their families has allowed nature to reclaim the place and that does not take long, thankfully.

Readers will know razor shells, the long slightly curved shells of bivalves with a cream-gold colour. Like all shells they are the homes of wild creatures and our common razorshell, *Ensis ensis* is a fast mover, burying itself in seconds if disturbed. Many inter-tidal populations have been devastated by over fishing and the species is in decline in many areas. Another story of our times. Hopefully one of these days declines will be in decline! Breeding occurs in the summer though larval settlement is not successful every year. Longevity is around 7-8 years.

A pair if ringed plovers put up just ahead of us. They may well be nesting here on the shingle area above the sand, or somewhat inland perhaps, in a dune slack. I would have expected to see injury feigning if there were eggs or young for plovers tend to draw would be predators, or other nuisance value disturbers of their peace, away from the site by pretending to be injured. A clever ploy.

Must put in a plea for people to keep to footpaths in the countryside especially at this vulnerable time when birds may be ground nesting and other creatures are in the midst of a busy breeding season. And plant life, too, needs our tender, loving care. It is a joy to wander the Westcountry just now but it does not take much to spoil the beauty we all love, and to cause harm by not thinking.

Five bullfinches together flitting across a woodland ride, a family out for a first outing probably, a fine sight. This, the bud picker or hoop, is a large finch, with both male and female handsomely coloured. We listened to their 'hoop-hoop' calls fading in the distance, a nice feeling of new life pervading the woods and countryside.

Three fox cubs at a well hidden earth are yowling and play fighting at dawn and dusk. They have a pleasant home amongst bluebells and herb robert, ferns and hazel. Oaks shelter them well and all in all their lives should be good if they are left alone. Food remains by the earth entrance show at least two brown rats caught this week, from the farm area a field or two away.

I have seen a barn owl hunting near the same farm, they also prizing rats and smaller mammals and possibly having young at this time. With natural predators about, the farm would seem to be rich in wildlife generally. In the distance perched on a hedge top a male yellowhammer is singing its ploughman's lunch song, 'a little bit of bread and no cheese.'

Somewhere nearby will be a nest on the ground among shrubby vegetation, maybe sheltered by a bush, or up in a dense bramble thicket. 3-6 eggs with spots and squiggles are incubated by the female for 2 weeks, then both adults feed the young for a further 2 weeks before they are fully fledged. Usually a second clutch is laid around July time.

Yellowhammers feed mainly on seeds of different kinds. They also take various insects, their larvae, spiders and worms especially when feeding young through the summer from May to August. A lovely bird of Westcountry farmland.

Large grass snake swimming across the pond, a good 75cms long. It slithered up over a log placed for the purpose of helping hapless creatures out of the water if they fall in. Willow and I watched the snake slide through the arum lilies and down under the huge elephant ear leaves of agapanthus, already in flower this year. It stayed there for a while but Willow's curiosity got the better of him and he made a move to oust it. 'No'. Says I and Willow stayed put. I want him to know all snakes are taboo, even harmless ones, then he will stay away from adders too. Willow learns fast, a bright dog.

However, the grass snake was looking for a sunny basking place I feel for it went on its way beneath the bottom fence and into the lane. A shriek and a rude exclamation told us its arrival in the lane coincided with a passer-by so I went outside. A woman was scurrying along at speed in the distance, the tail of the snake just disappearing amongst ramsons as it headed into the woods.

I was recently asked what good are snakes anyway? Well, we may as well ask that question about ourselves when we see the state the planet is in. Snakes have a place in the scheme of things, they help keep the rodent population in check by natural means and do us no harm really.

Grass snakes are egg-laying reptiles as most snakes are, whilst adders give birth to live young. Snakes have no external ears and cannot hear airborne sounds though they can pick up on vibrations and may respond to a forceful clapping of the hands I find. They have an inner ear and can detect vibrations through the bones of the skull.

Eleven wood mice! Most I have ever seen together at one time and all glossy coated in dark, rich brown. What a picture but I was working, clearing up and without a camera. As it is their retreat remains safe amongst ferns and old tree stumps, lots of hiding places and food.

Some books suggest wood mice are "strictly" nocturnal but that is not so for I frequently see them about by day if I am sitting quietly just observing. Pregnancies occur from April and with a gestation period of 25-26 days it is reasonable to assume 'my' eleven mice involved a family or two, with young weaned at about 18 days. It is said maximum age in the wild is probably 18-20 months, with peak numbers from July to September being usual. So a short life by our terms for this interesting little mouse.

Yesterday I was watching a nesting pair of hobbies high in a conifer, using a crow's old nest as their residence for this summer. Quite a scarce breeding species and a summer visitor the hobby is a scythe winged falcon beautiful to watch in flight. Watching one plunging and wheeling in flight after a large dragonfly, and hearing its mate calling 'kee-kee-kee' in piercing manner added a wildness to the day.

Eggs laid in June will take a month to hatch, with a further month or so to fledging of young. The hobby leaves us again in September so only one brood is raised each year.

The adult hobby is a competent hunter, catching most of its prey in flight. This comprises large insects and various small birds including swallows and martins which no doubt form part of its diet back in its African wintering quarters. Moving around with fresh food on the wing seems sensible enough.

With a quick flourish of stylish breast stroke a mole surfaced about 10ft (3m) in front of where we were sitting. Willow looked as astonished as I felt for though there was a row of molehills freshly raised I had not expected an emergence of this velvet clad earth thrower.

The breeding season is more or less as I write, being from March to May. It is likely that young moles are being looked after all over the countryside now in nests of grass, leaves and moss in underground dens.

The surfaced mole was not above ground for long, a quick flurry of activity and away back beneath the rich soil. Small the mole may be but powerful enough it is to excavate 10lbs of earth in 20mins. That's about 5kgs in new money. That's about the same rate as me in the garden these days.

I'd been watching a mistle thrush giving stick to a magpie that had been getting too close to its nest, the pied crow soon giving ground to the large, irate thrush. The nest is in the crook of a branch against the trunk. It is a bit conspicuous and using my binocular I could see at least two bits of paper in the construction. The thrushes probably read this column whilst incubating eggs, they seem pretty intelligent and discerning birds to me.

Mistle thrushes feed mainly on insects, insect larvae, spiders, snails and worms during spring and summer, and fruit and berries when available. I have known them with eggs in March and often a second brood is raised each year.

By the way I now know of two breeding pairs of yellow wagtails in North Devon so no doubt there are more around and about.

We have found an interesting but not uncommon fox situation wherein a barren vixen is helping another to find food for four cubs. It is pleasant to observe and all seem quite amicable and happy. There is a likelihood all are related with the helper fox more likely to be an aunt rather than just a nanny to the cubs, who look to be thriving.

Having two adults bringing food certainly makes life easier for the mother vixen and, too, the cubs. My guess is the other vixen did not move away from the area of her birth in the usual dispersal to find territory of her own, and eventually a mate, choosing instead to remain in safer homeland she knew.

Though dispersal is natural enough in mammals it is also hazardous even though they have reached maturity. Foxes normally disperse as yearlings, particularly male foxes though, as in the situation above, females may hold to the territory in which they were born.

Badgers differ from foxes in that most never disperse, both sexes often remaining at home. Even those that may disperse usually do so after two years of age. The perils facing wild animals are many and increase as our own population increases beyond all sensible bounds.

The habits of foxes to some extent depends on the type of habitat they live in. Those we are watching feed largely on rats and smaller mammals in summer and to a large extent on gulls in autumn and winter when roosts are large along the night time river banks. There is no doubt about it the brown rat is on the increase and has been for several years, with foxes helping to keep that situation in check, along with owls and other vitally necessary predators.

Photographed an otter by tree roots and dense vegetation, managing to get half a dozen shots off before it was away. It was close to water but I could not get that wanted classic shot with stream or river behind the animal. Not to worry, count your blessings and make the best of it gets a body through life. In the dappled sunlight the otter looked pale coloured, slender and beautiful. I reckon it was a female, perhaps an animal on the move through the woods, 'on dispersal' as it were, for somehow she looked young and did not give the impression of being a mother with cubs hidden somewhere.

But what a moment of joy, an otter lolloping through the trees on a beautiful sunny afternoon during the last bank holiday. Tourists everywhere, roads filled with vehicles and yours truly in a quiet little backwater sharing time with an otter. Now that's a privilege unforgettable.

The following day in this neck of the woods it began to rain quite steadily at 7.30am so I'd been in the right place at the right time. Westcountry weather, even with modern forecasting is often unpredictable. Where's that strip of seaweed and those fir cones I had in the porch? They were spot on.

But Willow took me for our early morning jaunt, wet and windy morning, a moorhen calling loudly and lovely brooklime promising a show of blooms any day now. Here the flowers are always dark blue but I often come across the paler blue form. Growing to about 2ft (60cms) tall Brooklime flowers from May to September, and is one of the speedwells.

And suddenly there is cuckoo spit everywhere, reminding us summertime is very much about insect life, hopefully in abundance. One sign of healthy countryside I reckon.

Lovely surprise, two days after seeing the black-headed cardinal beetles we found a group of the red-headed species wandering about the leaves of water figwort. The plant, larger than common figwort, has remarkably square stems and often has extra leaflets.

Both figworts were used in the treatment of scrofula, or King's evil, a tubercular disease which affects the neck glands. Thus the common figwort was also known as throat-wort. The leaves were used to treat gangrene, skin diseases, abscesses and toothache. Quite a plant then, and in Ireland regarded as the 'Queen of Herbs', due to its health giving properties.

Interestingly it was also used as a cosmetic, the distilled juice of the leaves said to remove skin blemishes on the face and hands. No wonder the cardinal beetles looked so well as they casually wandered about.

In fact, as with many conspicuously coloured insects the bright colouring exists to draw attention and warn off predators. Such colours often 'say', remember how bad the last one you ate tasted, leave me alone.

Look closely and you will see the unusual antennae are like hacksaw blades and serrated along the inner edge. Both species have yellowish, long, flat larvae with two prongs at the tail end, which live in dead wood and take three years to mature.

As for the meadow buttercups this year! Well the fields glow with them, particularly out of the sun if my eyes do not deceive me. Visitors to the Westcountry must be thinking how beautiful it is here, even in the rain, or should I say especially in the rain for the countryside can be very special in the wet. And as I keep saying, a good binocular opens your eyes to all that special beauty that is the south-west.

The hobbies I referred to in this column a while ago have chicks so the adults brought off a successful nesting, thus far at least. Must keep an eye on the outcome though I shall not spend much time on site as it draws attention. But it was very nice to see one adult on the nest edge and the other flying low along the route of a farm track in hazy sunshine.

Further up along the same valley common redstarts are feeding young and we also watched a male pied flycatcher for some time, splendid in his black and white plumage. Probably his brown and white mate was on eggs nearby in a tree hole nest, eggs of sky blue colour, usually seven to a clutch. Interestingly the redstart's eggs are much the same colour though those of the spotted flycatcher are generally a greenish white, spotted with brown. Incubation and fledging takes about a month all told.

It was the colour and flicking movement of the redstart's orange-red tail that gave away its location and made our lives easy when it came to identification. Red-steart it was, steart being an old word for tail.

Dog roses in full bloom. Is there a lovelier sight? I doubt it. Here in the lush green valley some bushes had the pale pink, some the much deeper hue, these and bramble flowers, along with buttercups as far as the eye could see stir ones emotions.

Willow chewed on grasses. Sometimes I will identify which ones are his favourite but for now just to stand and stare, to drink in the scene, listen to the bird songs and piping cries of fledglings, the song of the stream flowing over shining stones, bees and dragonflies everywhere. Tis ansome you.

Treecreeper family clambering up oaks in the heart of the woods. My cup runneth over with wonderful sightings and of course this time of year is quite perfect. It must be a relief for any adult wild creatures to see their young flying or running free and starting out in good weather with an abundance of food about. Raising a whole brood of several youngsters in one go is very hard work. Seeing seven treecreepers happily climbing tree trunks brings home to the observer how perilous life can be in the wild. Sunny day, lovely, but the weather forecast says probable heavy rain on its way, a very different world for young wild creatures who have to adapt rapidly to changing circumstances.

Dancing in a swarm around the trees and shrubs in the sun are many green longhorn moths. The casual observer may think they are midges or gnats but do take a closer look at this pretty moth. It is green and often shines red in certain lights, like shot-silk in a way. It is the males that swarm during April and through May and June, waiting for females to come out of hiding and mate. The moths, especially the males, have very long antennae.

Whatever happened to shot silk? It was all the rage at one time, like strangled satin.

A reader asked me what is Star Grass? I did not know but looking up I find it is spelt Starr Grass, with two Rs, and is a Lancashire name for marram grass. Marram is the common sand dune grass with far creeping rhizomes and sharply pointed leaves. It is often planted to fix the dunes to prevent them blowing away, and is wonderfully adapted to withstand dry conditions. Always glad to try and answer your queries folks.

As I write it is raining hard and I've just come in from taking me dug out, which in Deb'n means our dog Willow. However, the way June started out, dug out, the original form of a canoe, seems appropriate as our lane is awash with lovely sky reflecting puddles. You would not look silly sat in our lane with a fishing rod I can tell ee. There tis.

Insect life hidden under leaves, nature's umbrellas. I was glad of the canopy coming up through the woods but I enjoy rainy day walks anyway. I stopped at tracks in the mud, human boot prints and a dog's, already being washed away by the pelting rain, gwane t'other way yet Willow and I hadn't seen a soul. A few more further along, then two facing sideways coming out of our gate and I realised with a flash of early morning inspiration twas our own history in the mud. Conan Doyle would have been proud.

"What do you reckon Holmes?" says I to Willow, aware that with his collie ears wet he looked as if he has a deerstalker on. He put on his breakfast look so a towelling down was next, then his food and Rascal's, then a muggatee in that order. Look after your animal friends and they look after you.

Rascal our tabby wandered off into his igloo den so I knew the rain was in for the day. Our resident dunnocks were around feeding in the dry beneath our conifers. They have raised a family of five young and deserve a break as two or three broods in a summer are quite usual. Yes, also called hedge sparrows.

Saturday again already. Well, Zatturdee to us locals. Chap phoned and said he had seen the ghost of an otter on the River Lyn this week. I says woddee mean, a ghost? He said he and his wife had crossed the bridge down at Watersmeet and gone up towards Hoar Oak when he looked down and there was this big otter, all white in colour. His wife saw it too as it went up along the riverbank. He said then it went over to a big rock and was gone.

Naturally I asked what time of day twas and if ee'd ad ort stronger than tea. He laughed and said only coffee, and it was about 3pm in daylight though twas a cloudy, dull sort of day. He reckoned the sighting was a full five or six minutes by both his wife and himself and there was no doubt about it being an otter. The animal was over a metre long, he said, and he knew otters anyway.

Well there you go folks, a ghost story for the weekend. I have seen an all creamy coloured otter many years ago but albinism in otters is not common as far as I know.

The disappearing bit is not uncommon along such rivers and wild places and if an animal is aware of being watched it will often disappear with ease and you can search as you will.

I said what a pity you didn't get a photo. He said we did better than that, my wife filmed it on our camcorder. Dearie me, box of delights time so I've asked if they will let me see the results which he reckons are pretty good. I'm all excited. Will tell ee more fairly soon me dears. Fair made my day that did.

The spotted flycatcher in a hawthorn opposite back gate constantly sallies forth culling insects. It is an interesting bird to watch if you are not a fly on the wing. Its nest is in a hole in the nearest oak, curtained by ivy which provides shelter and food. The eggs and young should be safe from the magpies and carrion crows also nesting nearby, hole nesters being relatively secure.

A magpie landed on top-shed roof earlier and took half a rich tea biscuit I'd put out for the squirrel which eats from my hand, but wasn't around. The magpie dropped the hard biscuit into the bird drinking bowl, waited 10 seconds or so then removed it suitably dunked and flew off with it into the woods.

We have a family of song thrushes in the garden suddenly four young plus the two adults, a fine sight. They had hidden their nest quite well in our laurel hedge on the west side of the garden. The singing male's song has been quite beautiful late into the dusk, vying with the male chaffinch singing from the top of our ash tree, and our collared doves and wood pigeons who constantly bill and coo. Where do they find the energy? I am going to eat what they eat for a week to see if I have some kind of revival.

Robin has just found a newly built blackbird nest in what looks to be the most exposed spot possible and very ill chosen. Dog walkers pass within a foot or so all day long so we will keep an eye on it just out of caring and curiosity. Inexperienced birds, probably their first year of nesting and breeding is a likelihood. We all have to learn as we move along life's often bumpy pathway do we not.

For many years I have been saying that a closeness to nature is good for our health, as have many other naturalists, so it is good to see the recent Public Health White Paper agreeing. It calls for green spaces and the countryside to be prescribed as part of the perfect medicine. It is common sense really. We, you and I, are animals and a part of the natural world. It is a huge error to divorce ourselves from the fact and to isolate ourselves from our natural surroundings. It is criminal, in my view, to even consider constantly destroying the countryside and urbanising more and more of our tiny, overcrowded islands we know as Britain.

Great Britain it is, with an emphasis on 'Great' for we have such a beautiful country, such a superb and happy environment that I feel dismay that there are so many idiots about prepared to despoil it for greed and what ever else it is that kicks their tiny minds in gear.

Somewhere in the scripture it says the love of money is the root of all evil. Well, we all need money in order to survive, the system created for us to live in by the powers that be sees to that. But the love of nature is the root of all goodness and the antidote to ill health. Be in peaceful places folks, we have virtually free access to healthy living by not denying ourselves the natural world.

Just loving and nurturing plants in a garden removes stresses and anxiety. We really must embrace the natural world in a true, emotional sense to feel reality, we are part of it, always have been. Get wise, get loving, get into nature watching, get healthy.

Sow thistles 6 ft. tall and thick stemmed, powerful looking plants, also known as Milk Thistle and Silver & Gold. These are smooth sow thistles but there are others about including perennial, marsh and prickly. We are by a former garden site, the cottage long gone so we often find plants popping up from those days when conditions are right!

We had been along the Bradiford Valley near Barnstaple checking on pearl bordered fritillary butterflies and had found both the small, *Boloria selene*, and *B. euphrosune* flying together. The woods here, with their wide paths and violets in springtime provide good habitat for these insects, the two difficult to tell apart on the wing but once they settle you can identify them. In Cornwall I have found selene at coastal sites, and in North Devon near Woody Bay. August sees a second brood in exceptional years.

Along the waterway dippers are feeding young. This year they are at the end of an old mill leat where the leat water pours back into the parent stream over a 2 ft. high fall. Dippers have lived along the waterway for as long as I can remember and are always a joy to watch. With a territory of around half a mile, if you find dippers folks, you should be able to observe them with ease.

Young vacate the nest after 18 – 25 days though they will continue to be fed by their parent for some time afterwards. The young can usually dive proficiently for food before they can fly properly. They are quite differently plumaged than adults, being slate grey with a white chin and throat, and grey and white speckled underparts.

Birdwatching at this time of the year calls for careful observation as many young birds differ from the adults.

There on one of many ox-eye or moon daisies was a bright green beetle. A few of its kind were flying in the sunshine about the bank of vegetation constructed as part of a river flood defence scheme. The one perched was a male thick-legged flower beetle, *Oedemara nobilis*, its rear legs very thick indeed, a handy reference point. The legs of the female of the species are quite normal. It is an insect which frequents flowers in May and June, its larvae feeding in plant stems, though some species develop in dead wood.

We are having a grand time photographing insects this year and then reading up about them. One sees and learns something new every day, nature watching ever fascinating.

Talking of flowers Endymion went off down river to photograph the nodding thistle I mentioned recently and found a 'new' wildflower. It is grass vetchling, a plant of rough grassland, hedgebanks and wood edges, often on heavy, mildly acid soils. It is distinguished from all other legumes by the grass-like leaves, the flowers being snap-dragon-like in a way and very strongly pink. It is one of the great pea family, *Leguminosae*, characterized by the seeds being carried in a pod, or Legume, and the highly distinctive five petalled flowers.

The broad and often erect upper petal is the standard, the two narrower ones are the wings and the two central lower ones, which cover the stamens, are the keel. Good to find 'new' plants in the area you think you have been observing for many years. It has a body aware that you never know what lurks around the bend or over the next hedge. You just have to go and look, keep your eyes open and who knows? That is the fascination of nature watching.

Pale flax, Linum bienne, growing in a grassy area close to the saltmarshes, is a pretty sight and we can enjoy it in flower from May to September. It is not the flax grown by farmers though it serves to remind us just how important the flaxes have been for thousands of years. Today flax seeds are used in some foods for human consumption and moreso in cattle cake. The purified linseed oil is an ingredient of some varnishes, paints and putty.

Linen made from flax was used the world over and only lost ground to mass produced cotton since the 19th century. It was another flax that made the wrappings for Egyptian mummies of 5-6000 years ago and it was a well known plant in the Middle East long before the first Egyptian pyramids were built. Linen is still in vogue of course, for high quality cloth and writing paper.

Rather nice to sit and contemplate a plant, to appreciate and respect it and its kind for all they provide for us, and have done down through the centuries.

The pale flax waves its wiry stems in the breeze. It likes life near the sea, its lovely blue flowers with their finely pointed sepals found all around the Westcountry coast.

Homeward bound we found bugle in flower in a dell beneath ferns. It often forms large mats of intense blue but here it is growing in a row beside a narrow stream formed by several springs. A healing plant for all kinds of ailments and wounds bugle is a flower of damp woods and meadows, fairly common in the south-west. Early names include bugula, abuga and abija. Its scientific name is *Ajuga reptans* and you should find it in flower for a while longer. Ansome!

Jack tells me he is 85. He doesn't look it until he walks and then his sciatica shows. I can sympathise as back pain is dreadful when it is severe – I guess all pain is – and you have no obvious signs as to why you don't go through the day with a cheery look.

"Cheer up, it may never happen", people wisely say.

Jack and I have much in common including a love of nature. Oddly enough we both did our backs in as 1968 went into 1969. It only took seconds to do but what I mean is we each went through a series of treatment that did little good, months of it, and here we both are with increasing problems.

Jack is a lot older than I, of course, so was older when it happened. He'd tried to get a vehicle trailer out of mud in a gateway and it had not budged but his back 'went'. I did much the same.

We chuckled as we reminisced about our legs going numb in awkward places, of having to stand pretending we were enjoying the view until we can move again.

"I cried with pain sometimes, and if you're out for a walk on a nice day people don't understand", Jack said.

It is so. But as we agreed, here we both were, leaning on a gate with a view down to the river, birds everywhere, bees about the flowers, a contented pigeon cooing in the trees, in the beautiful Westcountry. Nature is truly a great healer. Of the spirits if not of bad backs. We agreed it would be good to start a Gate Leaners Club. Maybe we will.

Time to go. We both groaned aloud as we straightened up, then burst out laughing. Problem shared, problem halved.

Pearl bordered fritillary butterflies in a place we'd never seen them before. Quite interesting that but it could well link with this year's more abundant wild violets. The butterfly's food plant is the dog violet usually though any related violet seems to be suitable. It is not always easy to tell this insect and the small pearl bordered fritillary apart unless the two are together and you can obtain clear views of the underwings. As their flight seasons overlap it can be fun differentiating twixt the two.

We are fortunate here in the Westcountry to have both species about and I would put their status as scarce, with a need for some good May to July sunshine.

Saw my first marbled whites of the year on 26th June and quite a few ringlets too. What a day that was, with sweet cicely and fumitory blooming and many more pipistrelle bats flying in the evening as the sun set, more than we usually see that is.

There is always hope when it comes to nature and wildlife. I can't see the powers that be coming up with anything that reverses climate change now, or if it was ever an option. Too many people doing too many damaging things but it's my view that Nature has some surprises in store not too far ahead.

By then people 'at the top' will have changed and their predecessors will say "it is an inherited problem, not our fault folks", and on we will jolly well go. Not to worry. What we need to do is leave things as good as we possibly can for our descendants and that simply means doing our own bit every day. Endymion's 'Naturama' HAWS sheet is still available. HAWS, Help All Wildlife Survive. Send an sae please.

Wonderful perfume, the sweet, heady scent of wild privet which this year has spread remarkably well. Such a joy it is to see, too, its white flowers gracing the shrub better than I have ever seen it before. Local names include pivot, skerrish, skidgey and primprint for this, the *Ligustrum vulgare.* It was used against mouth and throat ulcers, a gargle with the juice and decoction of the leaves being effective.

It grows happily here with hawthorn, the two looking good together and just along the path is the blackthorn or sloe. Way back in the 16th century privet made fine hedges for gardens but I must say here in the wild with dunnocks, robins and wrens flitting about amongst it I was loathe to go home.

Sea arrowgrass, sea plantain and greater sea spurrey were much in evidence on the saltings. The first named may be found from May to September but may be easily overlooked. Sea plantain flowers brownish – pink with yellow anthers, in green spikes on unfurrowed stalks. The pink flowers of greater sea spurrey show a pale bluish tinge in the five petals, a lovely little flower of these tidal marshes.

A reader asks if swallows raise two broods in a year. They do usually, and three are not uncommon in good summers. They usually nest under cover of some kind, maybe on a rafter in an outbuilding or in a garage even, or tunnels and such. It is house martins which usually build nests under eaves of buildings. A friend has 8 pairs of house martins on her house, swallows in the barn, and grey wagtails in a roof gulley. Now that's a bird 'hotel' if ever there was, and the garden is full of birds too, five acres of it. Ansome!

A moth I am not used to seeing is flying in the woods behind our home and I am rather pleased as Endymion helped me plant several field maples there several years ago. The moth is the maple pug and it flies in July and August, wherever maple is established. Like most of the pug moths it is a tiny, quietly coloured insect though close up it is beautifully patterned as pugs tend to be.

We had been out observing foxglove pugs which fly from May to August. Its larva may be found in foxglove flowers during July and August, two exciting months for nature lovers.

Pug moths tend to be overlooked or glanced at in passing which is a pity as they are common moths in the main and there are many species. Many have English names relating to their foodplant, that is the plant or plants on which the larva feeds.

The maple pug is *Eupithecia inturbata*, the first name referring to size and markings. *Eu* is well or good, *pithekos*, a dwarf, from the attractive appearance and small size of the moths, whilst *inturbata* is from *interbatus*, not confused, from the well defined wing pattern.

The foxglove moth is *E. pulchellata*, from *pulchellus* for pretty little, and the moth certainly is one of the prettier of the pugs and often very common.

With July behind us already we might do worse than get down to some late summer intense nature watching before autumn springs upon us. Take it from me, as you get older and a bit slower you suddenly become aware of the rapid passing of time and you have not done half you want to do. Some will say relax, take it slow, it'll all be fine. I reckon panic like mad and get doing it is best.

❧❀☙

A huge wild cherry tree is down in the woods I grew up in as a boy but the fruit glows redly and there is obviously enough roots deep in the soil to keep the tree alive and thriving. The tree is also known as the Gean, which is also a surname in these parts.

The tree is found in many an oak wood where it stands out in spring when the white blossom blooms. It is still used as the root stock on which its relatives are grown to produce the more easily edible cherries.

'Cherry ripe, cherry ripe', the words of an old song would once have echoed in street markets and there were cherry picking Sundays in some parts of England.

The timber was used in fine furniture making. It is very attractive, a warm colour. We have a set of four cherry wood dining room chairs and lovely they are.

The fruit is used these days in syrups, cough medicines and liqueurs.

Willow squeezed in amongst the branches and vegetation growing up around the fallen tree. Quite a den in there. I could imagine foxes and other creatures taking shelter as, despite recent rains all felt snug and dry inside. Must remember it, should Willow and I get caught out in a downpour.

A barn owl flies through the woods amongst the trees, following a wide path running parallel with a stream. I reckon it has young to feed so is daylight hunting to make sure the youngsters are fed. What a wonderful sight as it passes by silently and slow, a ghost of a bird here in the woodland greenery on what is a dark and thundery day.

Must go home and get the paints out. High time I painted a masterpiece.

Man and dog along the lane, the dog unusually snapping at another coming in the opposite direction with its lady owner. Willow growled, waiting in case he was put into a position of defending our gateway by doing a chomping job.

"Dog days. He is always like this when it's dog days", the man said to the rather annoyed woman. I took Willow back into our garden and closed the gate. "Let em get sorted and gone, then we'll go out", I told him.

Dog days. Oddly enough it is this period of time to around mid August we call 'dog days'. But it is so named after Canis Major, the great Dog Star Sirius, that can be seen following the sun down as it sets at this time of year. In ancient Egypt, Sirius first appearance was eagerly sought for it predicted the vital flooding of the Nile river, the boon for agriculture, and was also the time of that culture's New Year.

A brief wait and the lane was empty, Willow swiftly out to mark territory and renew acquaintance with his world beyond the garden. At the end of the lane where one path leads down through the woods and another along the top of it were three small piles of grass. They were along the top route and pulled out, not the grass cuttings of someone who'd recently mown a lawn. Odd. Someone idling about perhaps, but once upon a time they would have marked the way gypsies might have gone, to tell others following. Patterans, trail markers, such as used to be left at crossroads for stragglers.

Willow sniffed each grass pile, then went along that path so I straggled after him. We had a marvellous sighting of three great spotted woodpeckers, a new family.

A flock of curlew cascaded in like brown and white bubbling, burbling water pouring onto the mud flats to spread out and hurriedly begin feeding. At about 22 ins., they are one of the largest wading birds and can be seen on estuaries, mudflats and marshland. A few pairs still nest in the Westcountry but less so than a couple of decades ago.

Curlew numbers will build up now, along with other waders, the breeding season for them over and done with. They will be with us from now to early spring, their various calls a treat to the ears as summer slowly but surely moves to autumn. Hard to believe the apparent speed with which spring and summer passes by.

Black-headed gulls, still in summer plumage have been moving back since late June and are about in good numbers. The gathering of their eggs for food a century ago had them become very rare and there was a real risk of extinction. But our changing ways brought about a change in their fortunes and the black-headed gull seems to be doing well here and across Europe. I have watched them at a breeding colony in Scotland, a place of feverish activity and liveliness.

Now they are part of the great Westcountry change-over as thousands of our summer visiting birds fatten up for vast migratory journeys away from our shores. In 8 weeks from now most will be gone, a sad moment I always feel, but they'll be back.

However, that's then and this is now. Time to get out to enjoy and absorb the remainder of summer. School holidays, families together and if it is nature watching that gives you pleasure it is for free and nowhere is better than here in the Westcountry, that is for sure.

Had to stand and stare for a while to let my eyes focus clearly on the upright smudge of grey-brown on a nest box lid in our back garden. 'Our' late summer visitation by a little owl had occurred yet again. The morning had begun quite well at 6 a.m. when I made a muggatee to carry down the path to back gate and unlock. I like to drink in the early morning woodland scene along with a strong Taylor's Yorkshire tea. And there staring from bright yellow eyes was the little owl, seemingly peaceful and happy in what is a secluded corner well sheltered from wind and rain.

Unlocking could wait. The owl was a welcome visitor and being mainly a dusk and dawn hunter it would welcome my absence. Willow hadn't seen the bird so we wandered away to the fernery area tended by Endymion. Various species fronds seem longer, the ferns more luxuriant this year but then, we have had our share of rain through June and into July. I remember seeing the first hedge brown, or gatekeeper butterfly back on July 6th and that was a wet and windy day, with the 5th even worse. Or better, if you love rainy days as much as I do.

Now there is a slight spattering of raindrops. Oh well, August rain brings honey and wine it is said. The bubbles on a cup of coffee will tell you about the weather. If they collect in the middle it will be fair, if around the sides as a ring, then expect rain. All over the place means changeable weather.

A young buzzard is calling from a tree branch in the woods. It isn't long off the nest, just the one again this year. Two youngsters in two years. Our pair of buzzards are not going in for big families.

To Lyme Regis in lovely Dorset to see purple emperor butterflies. Perfect timing and delightful woodland scenery not all that far from the Undercliffs. July and August are the months when the purple emperors fly, the females moving down from disporting themselves high over the oaks, to lay their eggs on sallow leaves. There isn't much obvious purple hue in the wings of the female but males look positively iridescent and show purple at some angles.

It is a powerful flyer and quite surprises the observer with its speed and when males come down, one sucking at the carcase of a dead crow, it is noticeable that the purple of the wings tends to show one side at a time. Fortunately buddleia was in full flower, the common purple one and two males rather took to that. A purple afternoon, stunningly beautiful. I almost mistook the first female purple emperor I saw for a white admiral.

Eggs are laid singly on the upper leaf surface of the sallow, or goat willow, the caterpillars living on a pad of silk along the leaf midrib and eating from the side of the leaf.

This very striking insect suffered hugely from collecting, often caught by being baited with putrefying meat, or 'sugared' trees. In the 1950s I was shown purple emperors in Herefordshire whilst in the RAF, along with masses of mistletoe in oakwoods there.

Thank goodness for a binocular, the males preferring the treetops, graceful, lovely insects but not easy to observe without visual aids.

Its scientific name is *Apatura iris*. It is probably from Apatao, to deceive, and oura, a tail, referring to the colour 'deception' mentioned above and the slightly elongate hindwing. Apaturia was also a title for the goddess Athene. Iris was the messenger of the gods and the personification of the rainbow, apt due to the iridescence of the male upperside.

We were watching a jay anting earlier today. An anting bird crouches in a mass of ants, holding its wings out to the ground to allow the ants to crawl over its plumage. Quite often it will pick up ants in its beak, putting them onto its feathers. The ants produce toxic chemicals to defend their colony and such poisons, being effective against other insects no doubt makes a useful insecticidal shampoo for the bird. Subsequent bathing and preening removed the dead insects. Makes one admire birds all the more doesn't it. What knowledge.

It is also interesting that birds do not use ants that sting even though such species are common. There are over 40 species of ants in Britain.

There is no doubt that jays have excellent memories and will find where most of the acorns they have hidden are. Back in the good old days when I took in sick and injured wildlife I had a sick jay for a while. With plenty of TLC the bird soon recovered. I eventually released it back into the wild even though it had a favourite perch in the garden it would make sway like a swing.

Many weeks later there was my friend Jay again, on its perch so out I went to chat to it, only to find there were four jays. It had brought its family, its mate and two youngsters and that brought a lump to my throat I can tell you. And that is memory, a caring for someone who had helped it become well. One of the loveliest moments of my very full life. I shall write a book about those days, some great and fascinating times. We are fortunate people to have so much that is beautiful and free.

The red deer calf born at the Sanctuary moves gently through the trees with his mother towards a group of others on bottom path. It is early morning.

Somewhere in the valley a cock crows and a farm dog barks. Somehow all feels right as watery sunshine breaks through the cloud cover to light the countless small spider webs festooning the vegetation as far as the eye can see.

A darker green line through dew laden grasses across the steep meadow shows where some animal, probably a fox, has made its way back into the woods, for the grass leans in our direction, a useful sign telling the way the creature was going. I know the fox family here have yet to fully disperse, two cubs of the year still at home with mum but it will not be long now before she chooses to be a lone vixen again. Of course, the track across the meadow may show where all three come home on a follow my leader basis as is often the case with fox families.

A chiff chaff calls from a hawthorn full of berries turning red. The bird often calls for a while to September end before it departs our shores, as so many summer visiting birds are already doing.

This year the wild arum berries turned scarlet very early hereabouts, from mid July in fact with many laid prone along paths and hedgerows before August came in. It is a striking looking plant in all its stages, from Parson in the Pulpit in early summer to Snakefood when the berries ripen.

It is going to be a sloe year. In Cornwall we found blackthorn trees laden with green fruit and I see the hedges in North Devon are equally full of promise.

A walk on the saltmarshes now may well turn up some interesting sightings with glasswort in flower to the end of September. The plant is also known as marsh samphire, a pioneer species of salt marshes which does well provided the seeds get exposure to air. This usually occurs near the high tide mark with rapid germination eventually forming colonies that hold silt and mud in their leaves and stems.

Glasswort leaves are fleshy scales, the dark green plant turning a yellow-green, then pink or red. Like rock samphire it is edible, and as its English name suggests was used for centuries in glass making.

To eat it, it can be lightly boiled or pickled in spiced vinegar. The pickle made from it is still produced along the North Sea coastal areas and is actually growing once more in popularity. Good, free natural food.

There are various glassworts, the one I am referring to being Perennial Glasswort, *Sarcocornia perennis*. In a way they resemble miniature cacti.

Again the webs of orb spiders glisten in the early light along the hedgerows, a sight I usually associate with October, and it is quite spectacular. These are opportunist spiders lying in wait for insects seeking food, the hunter hunted so to speak though the insects are seeking fruit. Though the webs look empty, somewhere a spider waits for its prey.

As we head into September man and beast come for their spoils in the hedgerows, seeking fruits and berries which are the end products of previous months of plant growth and blossoming. And I shall be off along the fields at day break picking mushrooms for a fresh breakfast fry up, or 'brunch' as some call the morning meal if it comes around midday time. Am glad I enjoy cooking.

Whether it is a large pond or small lake I am not sure but it is a fair old expanse of water and very beautiful. We go there with permission from the owners and are never disappointed whether tis rain or shine. Sometimes things get very special, often of an evening or well after sunset.

We had been watching the last damselflies putting themselves to bed on bankside vegetation when we saw large ripples spreading out across the water in our direction. The lake became alight with greens, browns and the golden orange of the sunset and I wondered if an otter was about. Up with the trusty binocular and there in the water, chin on the surface, slowly swimming with a powerful breast stroke, was a badger. I know badgers are good swimmers but this was not a river to cross, it was a lake with a path around it so I reckon the badger was swimming for pleasure and to cool off. Then no doubt it would wander up the hillside for a feed of earth worms and back home for a nap. This time of year badgers sort out clean bedding, a sort of spring clean in autumn.

To see the powerful animal swim to the bank to haul its glistening body from the water, splashes and rivulets running from it was a bonus to the day.

Lots of common blue butterflies about suddenly, feeders on clovers, medicks, trefoils and rest harrow it is a widespread species found in colonies. We watched them going to rest with their heads downwards on grass stems. There were many close together, four or five on some stems, then the sun dropped behind the hills and they were lost from sight in the swiftening darkness. Time for that welcome muggatee.

Lady of the Woods. A good name for the silver birch tree and the downy birch for they are graceful with slender branches, the former having the much whiter bark of the two. The downy birch has more variable bark from silvery grey to brown in colour and at a distance this is the only way to tell the two birches apart.

We found a lot of birch trees in Cornwall recently and it soon became obvious that the downy birch prefers the wetter soils whilst silver birch thrived on the drier land. Birch flowers are catkins with both sexes borne on the same tree. A Cornish woman who has birches all along the back of her garden told us she has siskins visit every winter, and once or twice, redpolls.

Pollen records have shown that the birch was the first trees, along with pines, to advance into the British Isles when the climate warmed following the last Ice Age. These days birch is found in most woodlands on poorer soils. It is the tree mostly associated with Fly Agaric, the striking red toadstool so well known from paintings with fairies and elves perched upon them. The fungus attaches to the tree's roots and both benefit from this association. Fly agaric speeds the entry of soil nutrients into the root system of the tree and in return receives sugars produced by the Tree. On older birch trees we may find the bracket fungus, a parasite feeding on the tree's sap but giving nothing in return. It is in fact a weakening association for the tree and it soon fails and perishes and the fungus continues to feed on the dead wood.

We also find witches broom, the bird's nest like growths, on some birches caused by either a fungus or a mite.

Looking out of a bedroom window in deepest Cornwall I watched a hedgehog slowly snuffle across the lawn towards a James Grieve and another apple tree. There were two apple halves in the grass, put there for resident blackbirds, one a bit bill battered. The hedgehog walked up to the less battered piece, sniffed it then rolled on it. I've seen it happen, the fuzzpig with all four legs in the air, just as folklore tells us. However, when the animal righted itself the apple portion remained on the grass as the hedgehog wandered off, the fruit not impaled, this time at any rate.

Maybe a bit of apple juice acts like self anointing does, ridding the animal of some of its parasites. Impaling, as recoded by many eye witnesses, may be more of a fluke than deliberate though it has to be said hedgehogs are peculiar creatures.

They are very agile and can climb fences with ease, and they swim very well. A thatcher told me he has found them hibernating in thatched roofs. Being able to swim well does not help them if they fall into plastic lined ponds so do put an 'escape' log or somesuch, or a shallow end to a garden pond. They can't get a grip on smooth plastic even though they can normally climb well.

'Our' hedgehog circled the lawn around the older apple tree several times at a fast gait. Why they do this is difficult to explain though I've seen them do so around another, in the mating season, in a smaller circle. They have been known to circle for up to two hours and on several nights in a row. Amazing.

"Bees must like yellow" my companion said as we watched them at evening primroses recently.

Actually bees see the flowers of this lovely plant as a purple colour, with bees and many other insects being sensitive to ultra violet light. Many flowers have honey guides, markings on the petals which attract insects to the nectar source. In the sand dunes where grows the evening primrose, the hearts ease has such petals as do other pansies. It is useful to remember many animals see quite differently to us, even the world of our cats said to be in shades of grey. But then, all colour and seeing is about light. Just look at a street scene with a row of cars under the orange glow of street lighting, then look again by day for the vast differences. Or sit at sunset deliberately focussing on colour all around to see it change and disappear.

The bees were busy, numerous and included honey bees. Some Osmia bees, *O. rufa* I think are usually found in old buildings, the barns and sheds here probably ideal for the species.

A fox ran out from beneath one shed. It is an odd building, leaning like the tower of Pisa but resting against a windswept hawthorn and only about 7 ft. in height. On wet, stormy days it is an eerie place but with plenty of wildlife including barn owls. The fox, small and thin, trotted away towards the ponds not far from the tidal river. It will find rabbits and smaller mammals as food. The marsh foxes are different than the farmland foxes. They seem rougher coated and leaner, a tougher life no doubt, for a fox anyway.

Several red admirals flew swiftly by on the wind, heading inland. About time a few arrived.

Dull day but a fine night for the Perseids. There must have been a lot of wishing and hoping on falling stars for a few days methinks. A helicopter was up and about at 2 a.m. and about still at 4 a.m., adding to the display of lights in the sky westwards from our vantage point.

Out on the lawn a tabby and white cat played with some prey species under an apple tree. Endymion opened a window and called, the cat picking up what looked to be a mouse and off it ran. An early morning prowler with its breakfast. The cat appears from time to time from a home elsewhere in the area. They like their own territories but know no boundaries when they fancy exploring.

As I write rain suddenly sweeps in over the hills and planned tasks in the garden go on the back burner. Two buzzards who have been walking about in a field in full view fly up into the stand of oaks and sycamores along a road edge, to shelter from a wetting. A flurry of sparrows rush for their hawthorn shelter to chatter about the day as a herd of 17 South Devon cattle make for a field corner as one.

Yesterday, clearing up debris along a shrubbery path we found a large rock hidden by ivy. Returning the rock as a visual feature in the garden-scape there were umpteen broken snail shells. A song thrush anvil, the birds having bred in the garden though now we see just one or two, a bit of dispersal having taken place. Well, the rock will be easier to use now so a good deed done for thrushes. A rushing sound in the bushes could be snails scurrying for cover. Collective nouns? Flurry of sparrows, scurry of snails. Ansome!

Two crows attacking another, possibly parents telling a young one it was time to be independent, part of summer for many creatures the dispersal of young. We had seen two foxes sitting on a hillside during the afternoon just looking about. In its way it was rather moving for us and we had to piece together our own view of what was happening. It makes sense that dispersal occurs during daylight hours for who would wander off to become a lone fox or lone anything else, in the dark?

We were sitting on a tree trunk just inside a gateway. The two foxes had appeared through an open gate across the way, left open to allow cattle to move twixt fields when they chose. Another fox had watched them for some five minutes from this open gate then wandered off. The two, which all my instincts tell me were this year's cubs sat together for a good half an hour until one rose, looked at its companion then trotted off following the hedgerow. The other watched it go then it, too, rose, went to the hedge and ate some blackberries. Foxes eat a lot of fruit and fungi.

Willow whined loudly, something he does occasionally when he wants to be on the move. The fox whirled, looking our way. I was using my binocular and felt I was looking straight into its amber eyes. Such a handsome animal. It was not perturbed by us, perhaps because we were seated, and trotted away in the opposite direction to its companion, pushing through rosebay willowherb on a bank and was gone.

And then there were none. They had not made a sound we could hear yet suddenly the field felt quiet and very empty. Time for our own dispersal homeward.

As I write it is sunny after heavy overnight rain and a pair of house martins are busy feeding young who are about ready to fly. They make a pleasing chirrupy watery sound each time mum or dad alights at the nest with food, a rapid intake of insects and away go the parents, white rumps flashing, to collect more food.

Cliff dwellers traditionally but nowadays seeing our own homes as ideal 'cliff faces', the guttering and eaves helping keep the worst of the weather from their remarkable nest. Two or three broods may be raised in a summer and sometimes young from an early brood will help feed later ones. Young may be in the nest from 21-24 days before flying so we can observe their progress and the wonderfully attentive parents with ease, make notes and sketches and do some real bird watching.

Hard to believe that as you read this they and many thousands of other birds will be winging to African wintering quarters to feed on the abundance of insects the British Isles lacks at this time of year.

The house sparrow flock is up to 15 birds, good news, and our travels around the countryside of late show the rural populations of the species is very good. Of course it is normal that there should be more birds about now following the breeding season but house sparrows have undoubtedly done very well hereabouts this summer.

A male kestrel perched briefly in the sparrow's favourite hawthorn tree, had a look around then flew on in low winnowing flight. The sparrows all flew to the ground, waiting for the falcon to move on then immediately returned to their perches. The kestrel was not hunting sparrows, more likely he was seeking small mammal prey or even a few beetles.

On the edge of Devon's border with Somerset we found a small colony of Tree Sparrows, one pair seemingly feeding a third brood, at a guess, for it is late in the breeding season. Some untidy looking birds were no doubt juveniles for they progressively moult all their plumage, including flight feathers, in late summer.

Recent reported increases of the species may be accurately assessed but I must say I rarely see tree sparrows in my wanderings in the countryside and doubt they are common in the Westcountry generally. It is a bird of open woodlands and orchards which feeds mainly on weed seeds but though one would think there is plenty of suitable habitat it is a species which has peculiar population fluctuations.

Sparrows are handsome birds and tree sparrows differ from house sparrows mainly in having all chestnut crowns whereas the latter has a grey crown, in the male, and no black cheek patches like the tree sparrow has.

Looking back to particularly good days of nature watching August 8th was sunny, warm and full of large and small white butterflies, scores of them passing along the valley. Then a call from Robin to say a clouded yellow on the saltings, a richly coloured one and always a prize to see. This migrant feeds on lucernes and clovers probing individual flowers with its curved tongue. The rapid flight and rich orange yellow colour of the typical clouded yellow renders the insect unmistakable as it wings in from southern Europe. You may see them, too, at knapweed and thistles.

It is possible that the autumn clouded yellows we see are from eggs laid by spring migrants to Britain. In this country it is unlikely any survive the cold, damp weather beyond November.

Seventeen buzzards in the air together, soaring over fields recently harvested, with some sending out the aroma of muck spreading blending nicely with that of new mown grass. The countryside is busy with farming activity as it should be, as a cockerel crows loudly, a sound that feels right.

Endymion points out a most peculiar patch of rainbow colours in a small cloud formation in an otherwise clear, sunny blue sky. The sunlight on moisture it must be, but an unusual sight.

Three ravens also explore the valley, 'pruck-prucking' in flight as they regularly patrol the area. Their nest this summer was in a stand of oak trees, half a dozen of them overlooking cattle pasture fields. Earlier a green woodpecker and a grey squirrel had briefly shared one of the oak branches, warming themselves in the sunshine. A stroll around the oaks showed at least three woodpecker-made holes at around 6-7 metres up in the trunks of these.

Common polypody fern growing atop some of the branches also does well in the rocky outcrop areas along with hard fern, hartstongue and spleenwort. Polypody has evergreen lance-shaped alternate pinnae or leaves, the fronds varying considerably in length depending on habitat. Look beneath them for the round sori in rows that start yellow but mature to bright orange in autumn. The sori are spore cases. On hartstongue ferns the sori are long, brown and in neat rows beneath the strap-like fronds, whilst on hard fern they will be found on either side of the pinnae's midrib.

For those interested in ferns the Westcountry really is first class with many species, a real joy with their lush greenness and grace. Spores fall to the soil to develop into small scale-like structures called prothalli which eventually give rise to the lovely adult fern.

Common jellyfish, a fair sized swarm of them drifting along the tideline, some up to 12 ins (30cms) across. Their purple-blue transparent bodies showed the horseshoe shaped violet reproductive organs and a close look revealed the frilly mouth tentacles. It is a bell shaped creature and by pulsating its body it propels itself slowly through the water. The stinging tentacles are not really a problem to humans and usually only stun small fish and crustaceans which are then pushed into the creatures mouth by the four frilly mouth tentacles.

The rather orange lion's mane jelly fish sometimes found around the Westcountry coast can deliver a painful sting.

The Portuguese man-of-war, also purple-blue in colour has tentacles that can be so long a bather getting stung by them may not see the body of the animal at all. It is not a true jellyfish and does not swim but just drifts with the wind and current. South westerly winds may drive this interesting creature ashore.

It does surprise me that so many people constantly ignore warnings on beaches, of the very obvious dangers of tides and the currents associated with them. Thank goodness for Air Sea Rescue and local lifeguards, but a swift kick up the backside, figuratively speaking, might reach the brains of folk who risk their own and others lives. Each year seems to see more foolish people than the previous one, suggesting evolution is not improving the human mind.

Land, air and water are the providers of life but when we choose to play and enjoy our leisure it needs to be with respect for our environment, not disrespect. I still look at the state of the tide and whether it is ebbing or flowing on everyday river jaunts with Willow. It pays to know.

The rather narrow looking tree in a hedge had a group of smaller ones shooting up like a miniature thicket around it, in a way like the Rhus does.

This was a wild pear though, *Pyrus pyraster*, its fruit sweet enough but it does rot quickly. The dark green glossy leaves have small teeth, not unlike those of the crab apple tree. I have found wild pear trees at wood edges too and suppose people made good use of the fruit at one time.

Crab apple trees may be found in hedges and thickets, too, in the Westcountry and you will find the fruit will take on a red 'blush' in autumn. It is the ancestor of Bramley's Seedling, Cox's Orange Pippin and several other tasty apples. Good to find these important ancient trees still surviving well in the wild, companions of oaks and ashes.

The Rhus is also known as Stag's Horn sumac and is common in gardens. From North America the Stag's horn name is soon obvious when the tree loses its foliage and one sees the widely spread branches, and velvet on new growth.

We had been following up on a lesser spotted woodpecker sighting, the little bird scarcely larger than a house sparrow and much more elusive than that bird. It was a buff capped female of the species so harder to find than the scarlet capped male. It is an elusive enough bird as it is, with its habit of living much of the time high in treetops and to get reasonably good views is always a joy. We were able to watch it a while longer and confirm its identity, then up into the oak canopy she flew. It is also known as the barred woodpecker from the smart black and white plumage pattern which is even more notable when the bird is in flight than when perched.

I'm a big fan of woodpeckers though I do wear a hat when they are about.

We were watching two meadow pipits, a common species often seen in open country and a resident species. It is often overlooked despite its being one of our commonest songbirds but that may be because it rarely visits gardens. Just a week or two ago someone pointed one out as a 'song thrush' and was taken aback when I corrected the error. But it is basically a little brown bird with a cream, dark streaked breast, usually seen on the ground.

The male's conspicuous song flight during the breeding season is heard as a series of slow, liquid notes when it 'parachutes' down from some 100 ft. (30m) high. On its way up it utters an accelerating series of 'pheet' notes quite unlike a song thrushes song. Now and through the winter the meadow pipit is often met with around the coast and on saltings.

Pipits are usually given their names indicating the type of habitat they frequent and the two others we have here are the resident rock pipit and the summer visiting tree pipit.

As I write this a sparrowhawk and buzzard are soaring together in a tight circle over the trees but that is all they are doing, no arguments or animosity and it just seems they are enjoying the sunshine. Robin came in rather quickly, he, Willow and Rascal landed on by scores of ants from the conifers they had been sitting under. Rascal made a dash for shelter under his favourite azaleas but Willow decided indoors was best. The ants were not on their usual August nuptial flights so much check it out to see if zummat very sweet, like me, was enticing them into the trees. We will find out and let you know for certain shortly dear readers.

Endymion found a tiny churchyard in a pretty village, backed by the lovely hornbeam tree. The pointed, toothed-edge leaves have parallel veins and the nuts are in clusters with leafy bracts at present, a unique feature of this tree. Back she went with her camera to take pictures and, whilst doing so, found a sweet chestnut in full fruit, also ideal for photographing. I believe it is rare to find so many hornbeams together and they may well have been planted to surround and shelter the attractive graveyard. Ansome! Hornbeams may be found in the wild but are only locally common. They grow to about 80ft (24m) in height and are rounded in shape.

A garden warbler was feeding in the hedge its quiet brown colouring camouflaging it well. It is an odd sort of English name as the bird is more a species of open woods and copses. As you read this many summer visiting warblers will be on their way back to Africa, the garden warbler included, having fattened up on berries and such first.

I notice quite a few oaks and sycamores have mildew on their leaves, a whitish bloom clearly visible, as readers will know. Oak mildew is often abundant on oaks in late summer and autumn and is of the True or Powdery Mildews and more like moulds which form a kind of white meal. Downy Mildews penetrate deep into their host plants and include the Onion Mildew which is so destructive. Mildews are small fungi mostly parasitic on the higher plants and found all over, including various indoor items kept in cupboards and drawers lacking air circulation.

There are many good fungi books including the recently published New Naturalist series book from Collins, publishers and titled 'Fungi'.

Rain drifting across the valley and hills, veiling distant landmarks, the sky a sombre grey but it is warm. Many waders in and shelduck and Canada geese numbers have increased considerably. We had been watching two Little Ringed plovers running and flying on the mudflats, a species I have not seen for a while, the last time being on the river Caen at Braunton. It is a smaller bird than the ringed plover as its English name tells us, and shows no wing bar in flight as the larger bird does. There is also a yellow eye ring and white line on the forehead to use as field identification guides. The little ringed plover also visits inland waters in summer.

Quite a few curlew in but no lapwing as yet. Several grey herons line the bank and the now common little egrets numbers are up to six just downstream of the town's main bridge. At least, it is the main bridge for the moment whilst the new downstream bridge is being built, a two year project.

Willow likes the saltings, the many scents exciting his doggy interest but thankfully he is not a 'roller' as some dogs are as there are one or two gull carcases lying about, and a dead sheep in a tidal gully. Amazing what dogs find to sniff at and learn from in the rain, you'd think all scents would be washed away.

"Klee-weet-tweet", the sudden cry of a green sandpiper precedes the dark looking wader's almost vertical rise into the air. We can see the white underparts, barred tail and the almost black underside to the wings as it rises. It is a lovely bird of around 9ins (23cm) but somehow always looks bigger, yet they will nest in old jays and blackbird nests in trees.

Robin has been photographing common darter dragonflies amongst other things. It is an insect we should see about through October, even into November and is one of the latest of the dragonflies to be seen on the wing. Look for them around patches of still water. The male's abdomen is red, the female's a yellow-brown when mature.

We still use our trusty single lens reflex (SLR) cameras and wont 'go digital' for a while yet. Colour transparencies are ideal for talks and I'm thinking of going back on to the insomnia cure circuit next year, with some fresh wildlife and folklore talks. Brace yourself folks.

Talking of late flying dragonflies I saw a lone male emperor only three days ago and found another expired on a flower bed. Don't normally see that species after August. Mind you, it is not unusual to see banded demoiselle damselflies to the end of September in the Westcountry. And skaters, too, are still about, wandering on the surface using four of their six legs which have hairy pads that trap air but repel water. Look for them to November then they will go into hibernation through the winter. Whirligig beetles will also be found right through October so plenty of time to study pond life still.

I love ponds and the life associated with them but such habitats must be treated with great respect. The trouble I got into as a lad going home with wet shoes and socks and why is it barbed wire is always an inch higher than your crutch is if standing on tiptoe with a leg either side? I invented the first fashion statement torn-at-the-knee trousers which are now so popularly expensive. Funny old world, buying ready torn clothing ennit.

Last day of the month. Can't believe it is October tomorrow but they say the months fly by quicker as you get older. And us folks with lots we want to do catch it hardest.

A stoat was in the garden again today and I saw it reach up quickly to catch a large white butterfly in its jaws. A bit of a surprise but I guess its meat to a smallish mammal. A brilliant hunter relying mainly on sound and smell it keeps rats, mice and rabbits in check throughout the year as it does not hibernate.

I have not seen many mink on my travels lately so think their numbers must have now evened out as tends to happen in nature, though they have also been shot or trapped as an unwanted alien in the countryside. A friend in Ireland tells me the mink is still a common sight there on its daytime forays along rivers and streams.

Same family of course, mink, stoats, weasels, otters and badgers, along with polecats and pine martens, all lithe swift moving carnivores. Saw a cream coloured ferret whilst at a Cornish wildlife haven recently so someone out rabbiting would have lost that I reckon. Well, there is plenty of food about for such an animal so it should be able to survive living in the wild for a few years and may well prefer that to captivity. There must be quite a few about now as I have seen a few myself over the years.

Polecats and pine martens are uncommon but the polecat ferret is fairly widespread and a hybrid of polecats and ferrets, which supports my point that quite a few of the latter must have gotten about. A reader in Wales sees polecats quite often.

It is pleasant to see chicory in full bloom, a splash of intense blue along the wayside long after many wildflowers have faded. The flowers open with the sun each morning and tend to close around mid-day so a useful plant if you are going to have a herb clock in the garden, as is scarlet pimpernel. Chicory was once used as animal fodder and the leaves eaten by us as a vegetable. Hereabouts chicory grows to about 20ins (50cms) but I have seen it along some roadsides, waving in the wind at around 4 ft tall.

A flock of about 20 fast flying teal flight in to where a freshwater pool links via an old sluice gate to the river. Teal fly very fast and spring vertically into the air when alarmed. They dabble in the shallows for small animals and plants. Males are attractively variegated in colour, the chestnut head with a green eye patch easily recognisable. Females are dark brown like so many ducks but look for the green wing patch or speculum. Our breeding numbers in Britain are greatly increased by winter migrants.

Great time of year now to go duck watching at inland waters and estuarine habitats. A good binocular makes for interesting times out of doors but as I've said before don't go over 10x magnification or you will lose field of view. Nort worse than finding your quarry only to have it fly out of vision never to be seen again.

Sighting of the week was a flock of over 30 sand martins flying against the wind, heading west down river to the sea, no doubt to join others as part of the great exodus from our shores to warmer winter climes with plenty of insects. They may well have night roosted here in the reed beds.

Moon showing through hawthorn, two tawny owls hunting as they have been each night recently, with a lot of noise. It is almost 1 a.m. and for some reason I am wide awake. Maybe it is the owl sounds and the wind in the trees but there is a restlessness in the very air that has me up and about. That is how I met a fox at closest quarters. Willow was fast asleep, his legs twitching in the dream chase special to dogs so I slipped quietly out into the back garden to sit by bottom shed, as one does at unearthly hours. By the time the luminous glow worms on my wrist watch said it was 2 a.m. I was in a doze but awake, the sound of Canada geese a rhythmic soothing murmur. Then two eyes lit by the moon stared at me from our back fence area and I froze as a fox moved stealthily toward me.

It dawned on me I must be a bulky dark shadow backed by a screen with a mass of mile-a-minute, seven feet high behind my seated figure. I remained still, the wind in my face. The fox edged closer, one foot, then another, its tread silent its eyes glowing with moonshine. Then I felt its nose nudge my left knee gently. I wanted to speak aloud to it. What to say? 'Hello fox', or 'nice evening', perhaps? But I was not going to cause the fox an unearned shock, or cause pandemonium.

It nudged me again then finding me unmoving and silent it turned to one side, staring into the garden's dark shadows. Then it trotted away along the path. I heard trellis move where it squeezed by and twas gone. That was it really.

Clearing out the old shrubbery today, no not trimming my beard, that comes under another heading. Hidden behind a buddleia and mahonia was a mass of raspberry canes in full fruit. Left them for the birds though one is always tempted by 'wild' fruit. Several wood mice did a bunk but the minor disturbance would have done them no harm. A sunny autumn afternoon would soon have them back in safe holes and I am sure my work provided them with new runs.

Half a dozen elephant hawk moth caterpillars moved sluggishly about on the ground. High time they pupated methinks, but they know what they are about. I could hear the plaintive 'hooeet' calls of a chiff chaff in the shrub area but could not get a sight of it. Lovely little warbler and usually the first to bring the coming Spring as well as being one of the last to leave us. A bird that loves England and is England in its way. The 'hooeet' call is clearer than that of the willow warbler I find.

The similar willow warbler moults completely, replacing its plumage twice a year which is unusual.

Shrubs and shrubberies are really good for wildlife and ours is over 30 years old now, so mature and thriving. I keep a narrow pathway through and it is a pleasure to stand quietly at different times of the day and night to see what is about. With ivy as ground cover in some areas and a few large rocks about it is a place of lizards, including slow worms, snails, small mammals, birds and many insects, as well as toads and frogs.

If you have some room in the garden do try a few shrubs if you feel trees will be too big one day.

Swamp elder, my old poacher friend Jack used to call it, the lovely guelder rose, a tree that does like wet ground and has berries somewhat similar to the elder. It grows well where I planted it at the Sanctuary, flourishing by the waterway along with sallow and alder. In fact Guelder Rose correctly refers to a form with sterile white flowers, sometimes known as the Snowball tree. The leaves, bark and berries of the guelder rose are poisonous to humans but I don't see many people wandering about eating any of these so not a problem really. It is one of the viburnums, several cultivated forms of which grace our gardens but give me *Viburnum opulus* every time. The snowball tree propagates by bending branches to the ground where they layer themselves into the soil.

On an outcrop at the sanctuary where grows an ancient yew there is also a thriving Bird cherry tree which gives an outstanding display of fragrant blossom in May. In days of yore I believe some previous landowner who loved trees did a fair bit of planting there and I am glad to say that tradition continues. I well recall planting 500 trees on the steep slope on a rainy day and was tired but delighted when the task was done. Now, years later, the benefits are obvious, the beauty and wildlife gain wonderful.

The cherry of this tree is rich in tannin so rather tart in taste. The fruit is used to flavour brandy and wine but is otherwise edible only to birds. The bark was once used to produce an infusion to make a tonic and as a sedative against upset stomachs. An old Scottish name for the tree is hag berry, probably from the Norse name of Heggr.

Wood sage still in flower but mostly over now as is to be expected. It was used widely in brewing a good ale and clarifies the beer very quickly. In the Channel Islands it was called Ambroise and used to both clear and add taste to a good glass of bitter. An old name is hind heel, the plant used for healing wounded deer. I know one or two country-folk who make a tea from leaves picked in spring before the plant flowers, as a remedy against rheumatism.

Here it is growing in a tall hedge but it is common in woods and along many a coastal pathway, gracefully beautiful with its pale green flowers borne in pairs towards the tips of stems. The stem is square and hairy, the leaves wrinkled and toothed. Wood sage is a member of the mint family, like other sages. Look for it in dry soils in a variety of habitats including dunes, heaths, grassy areas and woods.

Hawkweed in flower, the bright golden heads typical of the daisy family. This is *Hieracium umbellatum*, a common species which is necessary to know, as about 300 hawkweed species are recognised in Britain alone. The plant's botanical name means 'a hawk', from an old belief that hawks ate it to obtain the milky juice to sharpen their eyesight. Wonderful is country lore, my favourite aspect of natural history really. And who knows, maybe somewhere in the mists of time there are facts that bear this out.

As for the Daisy family it is huge anyway, embracing thistles, knapweeds, even the lovely dandelion, along with the tiny 'day's-eye' we all know so well in our lawns and other grassy places. Let's give thanks for all wild flowers for they certainly cheer our lives.

A large rabbit was crouched thumping the ground with a hind leg, a typical warning signal to others in the colony and with a whirling of white tails, or scuts, they all vanished down holes or into brambles. I knew it wasn't our presence for we had been watching them a while and Willow does not chase rabbits. Then out of the sun glided a buzzard on slightly raised wings to pass over us showing splayed primaries and beautiful plumage patterning. About 50 yards from us the raptor dropped behind a bramble brake and in a matter of seconds it rose with a largish mammal I took to be a rabbit that had not heard the warning. No. On looking through my binocular there was a fully grown rat hanging from the buzzard's talons.

There are quite a few about now, brown rats, breeding successfully at a number of farmland areas I know. Rabbits, too, are in good numbers but I have observed myxomatosis affecting them at some sites, a horrible disease.

Do rabbits drink? The question comes from a reader who often sees rabbits but has never observed them to drink. They do drink occasionally but usually obtain sufficient moisture from their intake of green food. Rabbits eat many green plants, tending to work in a semi-circle, most feeding occurring at night.

Rats will eat almost anything. A female brown rat may produce five litters in a year totalling around 50 young in all. These are able to breed at three months, with many young rats killed by foxes, owls, cats and other predators. Rats are active mainly at night and like to live near water. They are intelligent, wary creatures and clean and groom themselves constantly, but are at their worst when they get about human sewers.

Looking back, what a week the last week in September was. Chiff chaffs calling their autumn song along with the silver sound of robins, an absolute delight and though it seems long past now, to compare notes with an old nature watching acquaintance was useful and pleasant. It was also a time of scores of small tortoiseshell butterflies, a welcome sight as they outnumbered large white and red admiral butterflies. Such a marvellous change really as they have been very low in numbers for the past few years.

"My ice plants wuz late flowering, so us ev had a lot of they tortoiseshells in the garden. They loved the hydrangeas gwane over too, and basked a lot on the house walls and window seels. A lovely end to the summer boy."

Nice to be called "boy", and pronounced the Westcountry way, which I use myself but find unspellable. Ice plants, the sedum which attracts butterflies and other insects to garden flower borders.

Our big friendly toad has been about in the evenings. It has moved house to where bottom shed joins a row of raised stone slabs, perfect shelter and a good place for worms, insects and other small prey. Occasionally of an evening I see it flick its long tongue out from ambush. It is rooted at the front of the mouth and can be extended for about an inch (25mm).

We have worked out this toad must now be about 10 years of age, pretty good for in the wild, though toads are known to reach 20 years if all goes well. I love to see them about. They have an amiable sort of grin and such beautiful eyes. Endymion called 'ours' Moonwort, the name of the toad in her book "Down Ferny Lane". Ansome!

"Binoculars or telescopes?" a reader asks. He and his wife are keen on watching birds but want to spend a holiday on Exmoor watching deer. A good binocular is essential for nature watching especially if it is to become ones hobby with many hours spent in the field, or for garden watching. In my view a telescope is only a secondary item of equipment to have and if it really is a choice of one or the other then go for a binocular every time. There are some first class telescopes on the market now and they do seem to improve all the time, with some compact, lightweight models to be had. Whichever you buy you might consider rubber armour, and for a telescope a stout tripod.

Must say a holiday on Exmoor is a good idea at any time of year for there is always much to see and the scenery is superb. That goes for the Westcountry generally really, such a range of habitats and never any bad weather, just different kinds. Warm, dry clothing including footwear, a walking stick, and go for it.

Wearing greens, browns and greys helps with nature watching, or the more subdued camouflage clothing from Army & Navy surplus stores. Some camouflage clothing is too strikingly patterned for our countryside and even if some animal vision does not pick up too well on actual colours they quickly notice changes of tone and pattern.

As a walk leader for many years I found one of the biggest errors people make is that of wearing smooth soled shoes. I refused to take people in the end as too many were falling down on wet grassy terrain, then moaning about it despite proper advice on our itineraries. There tis, lessons learned and all that.

Soapwort in a hedge, unexpected in a way as I have not seen the plant in this neck of the woods all that often. It was growing at about one foot tall, the pink flowers in compact clusters a little like the garden sweet williams. The English name derives from the green parts of the plant being used to produce a lathery liquid used for washing wool. Indeed it may well be that the field where it now grows in the hedge was once used to grow the plant commercially. It flowers late, from August through October so there is time to seek it out. Soapwort has upright hairless stems and untoothed leaves with three or five veins.

We found rusty back fern, too, a fern of rocks and walls. It is the rusty colour of the mature scales on the underside of the fronds that identify and name this lovely fern. It is commonest in the south west and found in limestone crevices and the mortar of old walls. Here it was growing from a short length of stone wall with an old drinking trough against it, for cattle or horses.

A wren poked about for insects along the stony crevices. Always a favourite bird it was a pleasure just to stand and watch it search ceaselessly as is their way. A male blackbird landing nearby caused the wren to let rip with its loud scolding cry then both flew into hawthorns on either side of the stone wall.

I made a sketch of the rusty back for a future painting and on looking closely at detail found a male winter moth perched on a blackthorn branch poking through the hawthorn, with some nicely ripe sloes waiting for the picking. Not by me, I have not the time to go sloe gin making.

Chilly morning, mist heavy over the river and all is silent save for our footfalls and the song of a robin issuing from bushes festooned with gossamer spider webs. In the lane is the head of a fish, an odd sight here away from the river but possibly dropped by a gull flying over with its prize. There are three Greenbottle flies on it. For every loser there is a winner. Related to blowflies they lay their eggs on meat and dead animals but do not bother us in our homes as bluebottles do. By the way the bluebottles we see indoors looking for some egg laying site are females, males usually staying out of doors. Both are common and seen all year usually.

Some 5200 types of fly live in the British Isles and many can be a bit of a pest really though they have their purpose in Nature and as part of the Creation if one wants to think that way.

Several hoverflies still about. The ones about the lane are *Syrphus ribesii*, a species that mimics a wasp in its colouring. Its larvae consumes huge quantifies of aphids so are garden friendly. They may be seen about from April to November in all areas.

The hedge seems to be moving sideways. A couple of dozen warblers are on the move, leaving the country together, silently migrating southwards using the hedgerow as a final feeding up corridor. Wont be long now before redwings and fieldfares arrive as part of the winter visitor influx. Fieldfares bred in Cornwall this summer by the way.

Well tis Zatturdee dear readers and hopefully there'll be some nature watching on the go. Would love to know what treasures you find along the way, always glad to hear from readers.

Doing a bit of fence leaning last evening included watching a nuthatch and a tree creeper just a few feet away on a mossy oak, a real treat. However, seeing a grey squirrel carrying a toadstool along a horizontal tree branch was a surprise. Using my binocular I could see clearly as the squirrel carefully placed the fungi into a drey close to the tree trunk that had been used as a nursery drey many weeks ago. Back it then came, along the branch and down the trunk to the ground where it picked another toadstool, then repeated the journey to the drey and placed it inside again. The squirrel was caching fungi for a 'rainy day', a new sighting for me and really interesting. I know they cache nuts and acorns, it was the fungi storage that was new to me but some dried mushrooms or toadstools must be very useful in hard times.

I stayed on, watching two or three squirrels, noting which dreys they went to as the sun set. They did not enter the storage drey so I am convinced it is a chosen winter larder and will be visited by hungry grey squirrels during leaner times. Nice that.

But just as odd was the close to sighting of a shag at Penhill Point near Fremington in North Devon. It is a place where we always expect to see cormorants but is well inland from the sea and coastal shag country. Tis true, shags nest around our coast but on a pleasant day with no gales or bad weather it was a most unusual occurrence. However, shags are powerful flyers so I suppose an occasional inland sighting may be more common than one realises, for this the green cormorant as it is also known. It did not stay long, soon flying westward to the sea.

Standing on our back step adjoining the woods I was watching a common shrew which had appeared from an almost imperceptible narrow run in ground vegetation. The little pointed nosed creature bustled about poking its nose into every nook and cranny. Then it dislodged some wood lice, or chiggy pigs as we call them, from beneath a damp log. The shrew gave one a cursory sniff then picked it up in its jaws and crunched it up. A second wood louse followed the first and then the shrew was away. I doubt our paths will ever cross again.

Shrews need lots of food at short, regular intervals. This is in order to convert it into energy sufficient to keep its body temperature at around 37C (94F) as their body is so tiny that heat is swiftly lost. Thus a shrew must eat every two or three hours or it dies. Though feeding is around the clock cycle, most active feeding behaviour takes place at night.

Every day a common shrew has to consume almost its own weight in food. A female suckling her young needs about one and a half times her own weight. As for the smaller pigmy shrew, it needs even more food. They lose more heat because their surface area to volume ratio is more so they must eat over twice their own weight in a day to remain active.

At this time of year shrews have a thick coat to help them survive the winter though many may still die due to a lack of insect food. Many of those we see lying about in the countryside have simply starved to death. Survivors moult to their summer coat in April and May at the beginning of the breeding season. Interesting little characters are shrews.

Writing of the usefulness of keeping a diary yesterday and seeing a flock of 20 or so starlings this morning reminds me of how not so many years ago the starling was not such a common species in Britain. Gilbert White, the Selborne parson and naturalist wrote of his Hampshire area, that no known breeding records of starlings existed and he was certainly a faithful recorder.

In recent years starling numbers have dropped considerably yet again, following a period when they were abundant. A cyclical event? I think not. It is due to changes in agriculture, to pollution of the atmosphere from military activity such as bomb testing in other countries, to a general over abundance of human activity, and loss of habitat as the consequence. Just a point of view. Perhaps useful in a diary which is in its way a 'time capsule' for future generations.

But keeping a diary is best if you put too much in it rather than too little. A diary is usually thought of as a book of pages, with dates following the year but today tape recording, filming with camcorders, or ones own database on a computer are all available. I think all youngsters should be encouraged to become diarists, via school curriculums and at home. For them to know they are recording useful data for the future, on any subject, would help alleviate so called 'boredom'. A neighbour says only boring people get bored. An interesting observation.

Nature diaries have been proven to be useful. I believe a concentrated effort to have young diarists noting what they observe on virtually any matters would be enlightening and much of what is recorded might be acted upon for future gains.

Well tis Zatturdee again. I'm off out to make some notes and sketches.

Mole in the mist, the little creature gazing about from the top of its molehill as if it could see for miles. It is not often one sees a mole above ground but occasionally one strikes lucky and this was such a moment. Actually the whole scene was enchanting, the mist beautiful, trees showing as shadowy shapes, floating and magical.

In fact whether we could see 1000 yards is doubtful and that is how mist is termed, below this figure it is known as fog. It is caused by moisture which is constantly evaporating from soil and being given off by leaves of plants particularly on warm days. Some of the moisture is absorbed into the atmosphere especially at warm times when its capacity to hold water is greater.

When the air cools again the capacity lessens and any surplus moisture will condense out in the form of tiny water droplets suspended, as mist or fog. Mist frequently occurs over damp fields and inland waters and will lie longest in sheltered areas.

We walked to a landmark, measuring our strides pretty well and it was mist, not fog, using the above criteria. So, mole in the mist it was though the velvety animal was soon back into its hole, no doubt hunting earth worms, out of harm's way from foxes, owls, cats and dogs, its main predators.

In a field corner was an old rickety wagon, a harvest cart or wain. Ladder like ends to the wagon enabled hay to overhang and up to one and a half tons could be carried. This one had seen much better days but it made a useful sketch for a future painting. Always carry a notebook and pencil folks.

Cold, dark night, the woods lit by a half moon in a cloudless sky. Geese honking, foxes barking and the laughing calls of shelduck on the river instil magic into the winter's night much needed after a pretty tough old day. We had spent two hours picking up other people's litter in the woods and along the lane, a lot of glass included, as well as drink cans. Already two more cans lay out in the middle of green pool and that means rubber boots and a long stick. Stupid imbeciles these litter louts.

But now the calm, clear night and the sounds of wild creatures eased the angry nerve ends as we ambled casually along the wood path listening to oystercatchers and redshanks and just able to pick out the white of two little egrets on the riverbank. They often night roost in trees at the edge of the wood nearest the river.

Though most birdwatchers may not be tempted out at night birdwatching is a good winters pastime and as readers will know, bird feeders out now will tempt many species into the garden. But try a visit to a reservoir, you may well find the unusual amongst the more common species, be they gulls, ducks or geese. At least we don't have Arctic Circle type days when midwinter is total 24 hours of darkness.

The main thing is not to disturb animals in winter as they face many hardships and it is every bit as important to leave them be, as it is in the breeding season. Going out after a storm can be rewarding too, for some unusual species may be blown in by the winds. So make sure your Field Guide shows summer and winter plumage folks, they can vary a lot.

Ponds and streams may appear lifeless during the winter but take a look into clear water and you may observe small, tightly packed shoals of tiny fishes resting on the bottom or just swimming slowly about. As the body temperature of fishes is about the same as that of the water their body processes are working very slowly in cold winter weather. This means they do not need much energy to survive and, anyway, fishes do not usually feed during the winter. Small fish in such shoals may be sticklebacks, minnows or gudgeon.

It is now a time when ice may form on ponds. Though it may seem fun to a youngster to jump on ice and break it this will almost certainly harm the animals beneath the ice. The shock of ones weight hitting the ice is carried through the water and hits the animals almost as badly as if you had stamped directly on them. Fishes and frogs can easily be concussed or killed in this way. If you need to open a pond so that birds can drink from it use hot water, or better still have a separate bird bath.

And remember, never venture out on to the ice of a large area of water for it may suddenly collapse under you. Likewise, though winter nature watching at estuarine areas can be marvellous, wrap up warmly in layers of clothing and do know the tide times. They are in this newspaper.

Do please keep fresh water available during the winter in the garden. It is as important as food for many species and easy enough to provide. I am feeding the birds again now, began in late September and the birds flocked in. As I write I can see 14 species which isn't bad at all.

I looked down at my boots and a lace was undone. Now then if I was a superstitious sort then I'd walk nine paces before tying it, otherwise I'd be tying in bad luck for the rest of the day. Actually I did; not that I'm superstitious but having just doffed my hat to a lone magpie I wasn't about to chance it. I had to walk further than nine paces anyway so no problem and oddly enough there neatly placed by Mother Nature was a log to rest my foot on.

Dearie me it's nearly mid-November. Time to tell ee then that tis unlucky to receive new shoes or anything made of leather at Christmas according to old beliefs. And never put shoes on a table, nor store them higher than your own height.

Placing your shoes in the shape of a 'T' prevents cramp. Mind you tis really difficult walking like that.

Willow is superstitious. He never walks past a plate with biscuits on unless he pauses to look at me hopefully. He reckons sharing a digestive biscuit is lucky. It cheers us both up and keeps my weight down.

They say tis good luck to throw an old shoe after someone who is making a long journey or gwane on a new undertaking. I tried it on a chap who was gwane overseas. I caught'n a beauty up beside one ear. I eb'n 'eard from 'im since but I still laugh when I think about it. And a good laugh's like a tonic so twas lucky after all. The secret of life, well part of it, is to never take yourself too seriously. Looking in a mirror helps. And don't forget to drink your tea from a saucer, once, on a Saturday.

I was writing about cormorants recently and referred to the flightless species on the Galapagos Islands. There is a lichen there which typically grows on rocks and bark but which has also been found on the shells of living giant tortoises. That may seem quite amazing but there are lacewing flies in this country which cover themselves with lichen fragments deliberately to disguise themselves against the bark lichens on which they feed, and thus avoid predation.

I find that quite wonderful and of course it is also one way the lichen is helped, albeit inadvertently, to disperse. No doubt in its own ponderously elegant way the giant tortoise does its bit for lichen dispersal. Emphasising the fact that we live in a truly amazing world if we but take the time to test it with all our senses and respect the planet as our home. If only governments would do that!

The more one learns about lichens and fungi the more interesting it all becomes. For example we all know of Marmite, the spready food of sandwiches and gravy mixes, but few realise it is made from yeast extract, a fungi then, and began from barm, or spent brewer's yeast. This edible paste is now part of our own culture, and has been since its beginnings at Burton On Trent in 1902.

Strangely the fields where we usually gather mushrooms for a fry up, have none at all this autumn, most unusual. Walking out with Willow at crack of dawn and heading home with a feed or two added to dewy, gossamer mornings. Not to worry, there'll be other years God willing. And there's always laver.

Saw a robin feeding another on October 31st, Halloween, a lovely sight and both in mature plumage of course. Sunny days bring out the best in us.

Zatturdee again. The word spreads. Had a phone call from a Lympstone reader saying, "tis Zatturdee and us is evin a muggatee". Nice that. And a fellow we met on Dartmoor came over grinning and said "ansome to see ee", so the WMN readers don't all run when they see us coming and my picture shows me grey and bearded as I am, not a shot of me in my younger days as so many writers and others do. Mind you, grey and bearded and me only 27. Still, I had a tough paper round when I was a lad.

Dartmoor was as beautiful as ever and we had good views of five buzzards soaring near Tavistock, then ravens, a kestrel and a very high flock of 70 or so geese, possibly Brents or Canadas, dark against grey clouds.

We had a look at a bit of the old Southern Railway route that linked Plymouth with London. It went to Waterloo Station via Tavistock and Lydford. On the western side of the National Park there are a few bits to see, and it is interesting to explore the recent past of human activity on the moor along with the wildlife associated with it. There were Dartmoor ponies along the way, and a stoat intent on the trail of scent left by some creature.

Saw a stoat trip and roll down a river embankment this week. It got up just short of the river, looked around, chattered with annoyance then traipsed on upstream in typical bounding fashion. Stoats and Weasels on the scent of prey are usually so engrossed in the pursuit of a possible meal that they often have little or no idea of what or who they are passing by. Focussed via their noses, are such predators.

Six tabby cats wandering about. They looked in good condition, powerful, good coats, alert, bright eyed and bushy tailed. Definitely feral cats, a small colony, living where a farm joins the edge of the moor, Exmoor that is and a perfect place for plenty of shelter and food. There are a lot about in urban areas these days, in towns and cities, living wild, if not in the wild as we think of it.

Here on the moor, as they pace about watching us go by they look 'right', just as our native wild cats must have done years ago, or as they do in Scotland today. Tabby means 'water marked', and the beautiful coats of all tabbies, wild or domestic, surely look lovely. Seeing them with the background of beech hedges and open moorland beyond I was reminded of those in Hope Bourne's book, at Room Hill on Exmoor. They were wild and tabby as I recall.

One actually came quite close, slowly, staring eye to eye, the green-yellow eyes searching mine. Then at about 10 paces away it sat and began to wash its face with wetted paws as cats do. In the lone but not lonely world of its own head I was no threat but dismissed. It had its Exmoor life to lead. Somewhere nearby the feral cats will have dens. They are wild cats, no doubt about that, and there's plenty of rats and mice about.

It is good here. I was touched at seeing the cat family or colony and touched, too, by the track I was walking along. This ancient footpath was walked centuries ago by moorland people. It heads across the wild moor, into a coombe, crossing another towards the sea coast, part of our heritage, real history.

The cottage gardener was busy with his bonfire, the smell of smoke attracting me to investigate from a quarter of a mile away. Low pressure kept the smoke down but one could see it drifting through the hedgerow. I always check as in our area youngsters occasionally set fires to the woods which can get a hold in dry conditions.

The cottage owner came over to chat, keeping his eyes on the fire. "Secret to a good bonfire is to keep the centre fed. Never let them get hollow. I like a good burn up of rubbish once a year."

"Don't know about this severe winter we are promised. We were told 'twould be a drought summer like 1976 this year but that was a badly wrong prediction." He chuckled and said how millions of pounds spent on weather forecasting might be better deployed.

"But I shall have fine home grown sprouts this year so Christmas dinner will be a lot down to my garden. I've got a dozen pots which will have new potatoes too. And fruit home grown in the freezer, and jams my wife has already made. Most of this was lawn but I find I enjoy the garden more when I work to feed us both instead of mowing grass."

I felt hungry just listening to him. We chatted about proposed wind farms. He said it would help sometimes if they used up the wind before it got to his beans and peas. A man with a good sense of humour.

A mouse scampered along the path. "Look at that", he said, "And Burns wrote wonderful poetry about those wee beasties. Still he also won a prize for his flax seed. Did you know that?" I admitted I didn't.

Wild, wet and windy. We had plodded up over a very steep hill in cloggy mud and I was glad to have my trusty blackthorn walking stick as a third leg. Panting away I was glad of an excuse to admire the view, as breathtaking as the actual climb. Farmland with hedgerows, a river and way in the distance the shimmer of the sea. My companions and Willow were equally transfixed by the scene, the Westcountry at its best, laid before us as a sparkling winter landscape. The wind whistled through my beard, rain with it, as we watched a kestrel hovering below us, grey head into the wind, but seeking food, whilst ours was in a pack in the car a mile away.

He, the kestrel, for a grey head denotes a male of the species, brought the reality of natural history to the scene. The miles of fields, woods and hedges, the river and distant sea, all became part of a falcon's hunting area. Suddenly we know there are thousands, nay millions, of beetles and other insects, small mammals, larger wild creatures, all out there unseen by us, the predators and the prey, a Westcountry scene that is also a vast living, hunting and fishing area for a myriad of creatures. And the basis of all that is the plant life growing in and from the soil, or upon rocks and tree trunks, or in rivers, streams and the sea around the enchanted isles we are fortunate to live in.

I said to Endymion, who is striving to teach young people the wonders of Nature, all school children should be taken to such places and have the whole picture explained to them. It is the living 'classroom' that would best teach total respect for our environment.

Another badger funeral. I don't know if I'm lucky or unlucky to witness these hugely moving moments as the mix of feelings, sadness yet the privilege of sharing the moment has one welling up.

I have chanced upon three or four now, the recent one in a wood edge situation new to me but I promise you badgers are caring, loving animals who take care of their dead when they die at the sett. There were five badgers present on the slope under a bright gibbous moon, plus the one seeing to the burial and covering up of their dead relative or friend. The dignity and solemnity of the moment was quite overwhelming, staying at the surface of my own emotions until I felt I should mention it here.

What touched me most was that with the dead badger buried and covered back over with vegetation each of the five watching badgers went down to the grave, nosed it, nosed the one by the grave and slowly, yes reverently, ambled away into the wood. I stood there for ages against the trees. It seemed ages anyway, then suddenly the lone badger whirled and ran away into the tree shadows.

There tis. Country life. We are but a part of it and wherever we are at any given moment other little lives are going about their business. The Badger, *Meles meles*, our largest British mammalian carnivore and related to the otter, stoat and weasel. It is a wonderful animal with a lot about it we could do well to learn from methinks, an animal to be respectful of. Then, that is so with all creatures really, and plants too.

Have a lovely weekend folks. I'm off to plant some trees and shrubs. Ansome!

We'd gone out to do a stint at badger watching, as you do. That was the general plan, as best laid by mice and men but it rained so we ducked into a doorway half way up a steepish street. Rain on road and pavements, reflecting house and shop windows, the aroma of fish and chips, the hissing

of tyres from occasional passing vehicles, something cosy about it all even in a doorway outside.

Across the way were the high stone walls and imposing gateway and drive to what we knew is a very large house, hidden way back amongst trees. Beneath the huge firs, on top of the two high gate pillars was an owl, one on each.

"Goodness they are live owls", my friend said. I stared through the rain. They were. A pair of tawny owls staring back at us, silent but with an occasional shaking of rain-spotted feathers. In fact their shelter beneath the trees was every bit as good as our doorway, the birds obviously content on their chosen perches.

We sheltered thus for nigh on half an hour, the rain heavy, sweeping down the street, filling the gutters to the height of the kerb stones. Passing vehicles tossed water in what was almost bow waves now and not a soul walked by. But what company. The owls must have enjoyed their people watching. We surely enjoyed them.

When the rain ceased it was with reluctance we decided to move on homeward. Any badgers would be well tucked up in cosy setts. Not much would be stirring in country lairs and dens. A wave to the owls and we were heading back with pleasant memories.

Sinking almost up to my knees in a field beside a waterway I suddenly remembered how, as a lad, I'd play here where the water was often diverted across the meadow to irrigate it. We would see a stone dam made and water washing over the grass. I remember how once I thought it had been done by other boys so set about breaking down the dam to 'help' the farmer. He actually came along the bank soon after I started my demolition work and I received a clip around the ear.

Thus did I learn about the water meadow. And ear-ache.

Today in the right light you can see the hollow 'way' from the bank and across the field. Quite a lot of pink purslane grows there now, a low growing, pretty plant which is spreading in the wet area, and common in the Westcountry.

It is a relative of Spring Beauty though not obviously so visually until you look at the back of the flowers and find two sepals, not five as in chickweeds and spurreys. Spring Beauty reached us from the Pacific coast and was known in America as Indian Lettuce. At first glance the leaves are a bit like those of wall pennywort, I think.

Quite a bit of man's past methods of working with the environment here. A leat runs along one field edge, from the weir, and to old mills. An old bridge and a shippon were built from stone from a small woodland quarry where a fox now lives. These and the water meadow speak of hard but pleasurable work and the every day lives of men and women on the land.

Unplugging my booted leg from the boggy ground twas time to follow Willow homewards.

Quite an interesting sighting. Two trees together with main horizontal branches linked to form a sort of 'stage' overlooking a field. On one perched a buzzard, shoulders hunched in the rain, close against the tree trunk. Across the way from it, better sheltered amongst a curtain of ivy perched a tawny owl, eyes closed against the daylight. Along the way on branch three two crows chattered and swayed, watching us watching them. On branch four, a female kestrel was out on the tip of her branch, what a great cast for an avian 'play'. Wonderful.

We stood watching them for a while but the curtain of rain remained down, the five birds looking about once in a while, apart from the owl that is, but no hunting or scavenging was taking place. Not that that mattered one iota, to see all the birds standing in a row was very special indeed.

I suddenly remembered how very wet it was, and we were. It is at such moments you realise the superb waterproofing that feathers provide to a bird and why they need to preen them carefully into place each day. Even the few feathers on my hat keep that part of it drier than the rest. True.

Willow trotted all the more swiftly with his nose pointing homeward. Like dogs all over, when he's at home the first hint of a walk and he's at the door, when he is out he loves heading home.

A reader asks, why spring flowers in autumn and not in summer. Basically they live through days when a period of light doesn't exceed 12 hours, hours of darkness and rest being as important as the hours of light. Thus a warm autumn would better suit a spring flower wouldn't you say?

Why Reynard for foxes, presumably only of the male gender, and no name for the vixen along the same lines? I asked the question of a few acquaintances and then by sheer serendipity found it whilst reading a country book. Reynard, it says is from reginhard, wise in counsel and very cunning (regin) and 'ard' or 'art' as male.

Thus we have mallard for the drake wild duck even though the name applies these days to the male and female of the species.

There are quite a few mallard about at present, the males with shining bottle green head and neck and pearly grey breast. Look closely, too, at the females, no less beautiful in their quiet browns. Lovely colour, brown; Mother Nature knows best how to use it.

We saw a flock of teal flighting in to a pond beside some sheltering coverts the other evening. Talk about fast flyers, little wings whipping the air. They are dabbling duck, usually found along shorelines of boggy pools and lakes especially in winter when resident numbers are increased by migrants. I find their mix of calls soothing and peaceful, the chirruping of the females and the fluting calls of males blending in a pleasing little pastoral symphony.

The apt collective name, a spring of teal, tells us of the almost vertical, rapid take off.

On my birthday each year, at All Souls' College, Oxford, a Lord Mallard is elected to 'hunt the mallard' through each chamber of the College. It is a fun moment in the year begun when a massive mallard was found trapped in a drain when the College was first built.

A pair of stonechats has moved from their usual favourite area to reside closer to our place. No, nort to do with my charm or my beard as potential nesting habitat, it's because the new downstream bridge building is causing quite a lot of wildlife to shift. Down in Cornwall the stonechat is also known as a furze chitter, a chat that is often found around furze or gorse.

Wordsworth called it a restless bird which is fair enough for it rarely stays still more than a few seconds. Mind you, males often perch constantly around nest habitat on top of bushes, making photography relatively easy. I'm going to stick my neck out and add fir chat to the list of habitat names as the bird has certainly taken well to young forestry habitat in recent years.

Each day we see a number of meadow pipits flying low then perching to feed and on again along the river bank. There are ten or a dozen in all and I haven't found out yet where they go, or how far their feeding area is. An old belief says that the pipit is always trying to get into the cuckoo's mouth and if it was to succeed the end of the world would come.

This superstition comes about from country folk seeing pipits feeding young cuckoos at the nest, thrusting their heads into the much larger birds gape, to feed it. The meadow pipit, like the dunnocks, commonly plays host to the cuckoo though the latter is now much rarer than it used to be.

How times change. I never dreamed the time would come when hearing a cuckoo would be an uncommon occasion but the bird has gone missing from many of its previous haunts.

Doing some serious tree hunting this week folks as I botched the identification of some leaves sent in the post to me recently. They did arrive brown and crushed up but I don't like to misidentify.

Up behind my hut are some yews, one extremely old I would say. Though it is sometimes referred to as the English yew, which it is if it is native to England I suppose, it is in fact found wild from western Ireland eastwards to the Himalayas. It is found from the lowlands of Scandinavia to Greece, Sicily, Spain and North Africa so quite a range for this lovely tree species.

Like the yew at the sanctuary, the tree is often wider than it is tall and typically its dense foliage shades out other plant growth. I must say I much prefer the yew trees left to their natural shape rather than clipped and topiaried.

As to its poison content the yew is notorious though I am inclined to think that it is more poisonous in some areas than in others. A farmer in Dumfries told me his cattle eat it with no ill effect. He said animals differ in their resistance to poison and, "everyone knows the yew's toxicity varies seasonally, mainly according to whether the sap is rising or not". However, the safe way is to keep its foliage away from animals and the seeds well away from children. The bright red, fleshy aril containing the seed is not poisonous and is loved by birds.

It is safe to say a yew may live to between 500-1000 years of age, maybe more. No surprise then that it is a symbol of everlasting life with sprigs of it buried with the dead and a tree associated with both pagan and Christian beliefs.

We have had green lacewings coming to light on the windows. The slim green bodies and transparent wings make them quite beautiful against the light. These are just over half an inch in length and I had thought they would have hibernated way back in early October and we wouldn't have seen the full insect about so late in the year. Trouble is we are used to two overlapping generations in late spring and summer but one wonders, has there been a third generation this year?

I see from the diary that there were six on the glass of the kitchen door on the night of November 24th. Twas pouring with rain, had been most of the day, and these charming insects were dry and safe enough there in the night. Lacewings especially attack aphids.

Our light-seeking lacewings were no doubt seeking to come indoors to hibernate and during the winter they turn red, then become green again in spring. Larva may cover their backs with aphid skins so as to look like a piece of rubbish and thus escape predation by insect eating birds. I call that intelligence, don't you? The world of insects is amazing.

But a few days ago a great spotted woodpecker arrived on the bird table seeking peanuts which had 'run out'. I was debating whether to put out more or wait til the morrow when I saw the bird trying to reach its beak beneath the foot of a ladder I put up from fence to table for creatures wanting to use it as a bridge. Getting my binocular I was surprised to see the bird pick up a twig of about three inches long and thrust it into the tiny gap, push out two peanuts and take them away. Tool using!

Leading a guided walk based on Henry Williamson's *Tarka the Otter*, shock of shocks our little group saw an otter in the Barnstaple Yeo just as I was explaining that part of the story. At such moments you try to look nonchalant, as if it was all timed to perfection but I was grinning from ear to ear with delight. Indeed from ear to there as well. True it was raining and photography was not on but the otter did its 'V' shaped wake thing then a few whirling dives towards us, under the bridge we stood on and went upstream.

What a walk! We'd only been out half an hour or so in a more urban habitat than usual at the edge of town, so a magic box of a walk really, perfect for a walk leader. Awestruck silence, just raindrops pattering and the splashing of an otter. I think the walkers will come back, it is a pretty little place.

Some walks go like that. Let's face it, it is difficult to walk for a mile or two in the Westcountry without having good sightings whatever the weather. Try it. Walk a mile without seeing interesting wildlife and you'd have to be blindfolded. I could write a different nature story from our back gate every day. Now there's a book. A year from our back gate. 365 tales. Any publishers out there?

I went home, made a muggatee and told the gang how Tarka's descendent was there on cue. Good chap H.W. If he had not gotten out his pen in 1923 or so our little group would not have seen that otter. 80 odd years or so later and the story came to life in its own way. Ansome!

Boots or shoes? There are excellent examples of both in the shops these days, all with soles that grip, and waterproofing that makes for comfortable walking. A lot depends on the terrain you regularly walk over and in the main I suggest boots are best every time for they do help prevent bruised or pricked ankles and provide firmer footing.

Boots must be waterproof so look for a wide welt and long tongue. I always carry spare laces. I have leather boots and those ankle length 'wellington' type rubber footed boots which I must say are very comfortable and keep me dry all day in soaking grasslands. Actual full length rubber boots, the good old fashioned wellie, really are dry and comfortable these days. Hunter and those from Hawkshead are shaped and really good value.

Wet feet are awful things to lug around with you on a long walk, and for extra comfort invest in some thick, warm socks. Touch wood, in all my years of country walking I've never had a blister so I must be doing it right.

Hats yes. A good tweed, brimmed hat that fits snug and does not blow off in high winds, or a wider brimmed bush hat is good. I find the latter keeps rain off my spectacles. Ansome!

Coats need to be roomy and waterproof. Some 'sweat' and are a nuisance for you may get wetter inside than out. And when it comes to shirts and jumpers, cotton and wool are much better than acrylics I reckon. I did a two hours plod in pouring rain earlier. It did not stop and the wind was high. We did the open marshes, muddy tracks and waterlogged lanes. I was dry as a bone when I took off the outer gear.

# Epilogue

Who would have guessed it? When Janet Wooster of the *Western Morning News* took me on to write "Nature Watch" six days a week, every week, all those years ago it was a dream come true. To write about nature, wildlife, the countryside, in such a way is a freedom for one's spirit and, hopefully, brings a gain to wildlife conservation. So yes, thank you WMN for all these years and, I hope, many more.

And thanks to the gang at home who help and tolerate the muggatees and all that goes to nature watching in fields, woods, hedgerows, riverbanks and coastal habitats throughout the Westcountry. Fabulous is the word and I owe them and our dogs and cats for joining in with it all.

Rascal followed Jasper and several other cats and passed over in February 2011. Willow, our collie cross is still with us. Ansome! And very much part and parcel of our nature walks.

So *Nature Watch 3* then, thanks to Halsgrove Publishers as ever, and thanks to all the readers out there. All being well, more to come folks …

**Trevor Beer, MBE**
**North Devon 2011**